Owing to the influx of digital technologies, rapidly changing global dynamics, and the COVID-led transformation, human capital has assumed an ever-important role. Be it a firm or a country, without effectively capitalizing human capital, the goals of economic growth and development can never be achieved. The book in hand provides an-in-depth understanding of the role of human capital in the present era and offers practical strategies to develop and capitalize human capital for growth. The book is a must read premier for all stakeholders alike including employers, academicians, students, faculty members and researchers.
Talib Syed Karim, *President, Institute of Business Management (IoBM), Karachi; President, Management Association of Pakistan (MAP); President, Association of Management Development Institutions of Pakistan (AMDIP)*

Organizations competing in recent times demand to be highly resilient, which is only possible by the way of developing the right mix of human capitals i.e. education, health care, housing etc. The present book can play an instrumental role in helping organizations to do that. The approach of the book is very simple and to the point with some elaborative examples, making it a wonderful read for business managers, researchers and academics. Particularly, the intellectual discussion on the difference between human capital and human capital resources and its linkage with cutting-edge technologies make this book unique.
Prof. Dr. Shawkat Hammoudeh, *Drexel University, USA*

I could say without any shadow of doubt that Dr. Shahbaz and colleagues have made a significant contribution by writing this book. I would strongly recommend this book to those interested to know multifaceted roles of human capital at micro level.
Dr. Muhammad Ali Nasir, *Associate Professor, University of Huddersfield, United Kingdom*

The work on human capital has entered into a new sphere where the scholars and practitioners are looking forward to combine human and artificial intelligence to get the ground-breaking results. In this vein, present book is a timely contribution, covering diverse aspects of human capital and their linkages. I would strongly recommend researchers, practitioners, and policy makers to benefit from the is book. Particularly, I would like to mention the concept of 'xaptation', which provides deeper insight about the role of human capital in firm performance.
Prof. Phil Allmendinger, *Cambridge University, United Kingdom*

Human Capital, Innovation, and Disruptive Digital Technology

Human capital appears to be at the core of business strategies helping firms to recover from the catastrophic effects of COVID-19 and bounce back effectively. This book provides a diverse view of the human capital, and its multifaceted role and application in an organization. The book also offers a comprehensive analysis on the role of human capital in Industry 4.0, firm internationalization, and organizational ambidexterity and outlines strategies for the firm to improve its human capital readiness, keeping in view the contemporary business dynamics. A very simple and focused approach has been adopted throughout the book to make it readable for the people from the diverse fields. The book also focuses upon the conceptualizations and measurements of human capital in order to offer conceptual clarity of human capital to readers. A central focus of the book is how human capital interacts with and complements other organizational resources and technological developments.

The book will be extremely useful for top-tier managers, researchers, academicians, consultants, and practitioners interested in gaining a current, relevant, and diverse perspective on human capital, its dimensions, and development.

Muhammad Shujaat Mubarik is a Professor and Dean, College of Business Management at Institute of Business Management, Karachi, Pakistan.

Muhammad Shahbaz is a Professor of Economics at the School of Management and Economics, Beijing Institute of Technology, China.

Qaisar Abbas is Chief of Research Division, CAREC Institute, Urumqi, China.

Routledge Studies in Management, Organizations and Society

This series presents innovative work grounded in new realities, addressing issues crucial to an understanding of the contemporary world. This is the world of organized societies, where boundaries between formal and informal, public and private, local and global organizations have been displaced or have vanished, along with other nineteenth century dichotomies and oppositions. Management, apart from becoming a specialized profession for a growing number of people, is an everyday activity for most members of modern societies.

Similarly, at the level of enquiry, culture and technology, and literature and economics, can no longer be conceived as isolated intellectual fields; conventional canons and established mainstreams are contested. *Management, Organizations and Society* addresses these contemporary dynamics of transformation in a manner that transcends disciplinary boundaries, with books that will appeal to researchers, students and practitioners alike.

Recent titles in this series include:
Corporate Social Responsibility and Sustainability
From Values to Impact
Edited by Katarzyna Bachnik, Magdalena Kaźmierczak, Magdalena Rojek-Nowosielska, Magdalena Stefańska and Justyna Szumniak-Samolej

The Dark Side of Organizational Behavior
Examining Undesirable Aspects of Organizational Life
Edited by H. Cenk Sözen and H. Nejat Basım

Workplace Monitoring and Technology
Jacek Woźniak

The Impact of Corporate Social Responsibility
Corporate Activities, the Environment and Society
Edited by Robert Kudłak, Ralf Barkemeyer, Lutz Preuss and Anna Heikkinen

Human Capital, Innovation, and Disruptive Digital Technology

A Multidimensional Perspective

Muhammad Shujaat Mubarik,
Muhammad Shahbaz, and
Qaisar Abbas

LONDON AND NEW YORK

First published 2023
by Routledge
605 Third Avenue, New York, NY 10158

and by Routledge
4 Park Square, Milton Park, Abingdon, Oxon, OX14 4RN

Routledge is an imprint of the Taylor & Francis Group, an informa business

© 2023 Muhammad Shujaat Mubarik, Muhammad Shahbaz and Qaisar Abbas

The right of Muhammad Shujaat Mubarik, Muhammad Shahbaz and Qaisar Abbas to be identified as authors of this work has been asserted in accordance with sections 77 and 78 of the Copyright, Designs and Patents Act 1988.

All rights reserved. No part of this book may be reprinted or reproduced or utilised in any form or by any electronic, mechanical, or other means, now known or hereafter invented, including photocopying and recording, or in any information storage or retrieval system, without permission in writing from the publishers.

Trademark notice: Product or corporate names may be trademarks or registered trademarks, and are used only for identification and explanation without intent to infringe.

Library of Congress Cataloguing-in-Publication Data
Names: Mubarik, Muhammad Shujaat, author. | Shahbaz, Muhammad, author. | Abbas, Qaisar, 1969- author.
Title: Human capital, innovation, and disruptive digital technology: a multidimensional perspective / Muhammad Shujaat Mubarik, Muhammad Shahbaz and Qaisar Abbas.
Description: New York, NY: Routledge, 2023. | Includes bibliographical references and index.
Identifiers: LCCN 2022015178 | ISBN 9781032050799 (hardback) | ISBN 9781032050805 (paperback) | ISBN 9781003195894 (ebook)
Subjects: LCSH: Human capital--Management. | Manpower planning. | Personnel management.
Classification: LCC HD4904.7.M83 2023 | DDC 658.3--dc23/eng/ 20220408
LC record available at https://lccn.loc.gov/2022015178

ISBN: 978-1-032-05079-9 (hbk)
ISBN: 978-1-032-05080-5 (pbk)
ISBN: 978-1-003-19589-4 (ebk)

DOI: 10.4324/9781003195894

Typeset in Bembo
by MPS Limited, Dehradun

Dedicated to my father, Mubarik Ahmed, whose unconditional support has always been a guiding force for me during all the heavy odds of life; my mother who served as a shade over my head against the scorching noontimes of struggle; my daughter Emaan, and my son Hadi who have been personification optimism and redemption for me......Muhammad Shujaat Mubarik

Dedicated to my mother for her love and prayers, and to Azil, my son, who is a greatest source of inspiration for me......Muhammad Shahbaz

To my parents, who made me what I am today......
Dr. Qaisar Abbas

Contents

List of Figures	xi
List of Tables	xii
Author Biographies	xiii
Foreword	xv
Preface	xvii
Acknowledgements	xix

1	Human Capital: Evolution and Dimensions	1
2	Human Capital: Gauging the Ungauged	12
3	Human Capital or Human Capital Readiness: What Matters for Performance?	25
4	Human Capital and Internationalization	37
5	Human Capital Development Strategies and Ambidextrous Learning	50
6	Fathered Alone Raised Together: A Discourse on the Role of Human Capital and Human Capital Resource Leading to Innovative Work Behaviour of Employees	65
7	Beyond Conventional Human Capital: Behavioural Human Capital in Driving Firms' Absorptive Capacity and Innovation	79
8	Human Capital in Cross-border Mergers and Acquisitions: An Exaptation Perspective	99

x *Contents*

9 Human Capital, Technological Capabilities, and
   Productivity: Firm-Level Evidence   111

10 Human Capital for Fourth Industrial Revolution:
   Human Capital 4.0   132

   Index   151

Figures

3.1	Objectives Focused Roles-Division	30
3.2	Mapping Human Capital	31
3.3	Human Capital Readiness Framework	33
3.4	Human Capital Readiness Spectrum	34
4.1	Human Capital and Internalization Framework	43
4.2	Human Capital Requirement Model	44
4.3	AHP Hierarchy of Human Capital Dimensions	45
5.1	TMS Framework	54
5.2	Acquisition Process	55
5.3	Learning Process	60
5.4	HCDS-led-organizational Ambidexterity Model	62
6.1	Task Complexity—Low vs. High	70
6.2	Linking HC and HCR with IWB	76
7.1	Behavioural Human Capital	80
7.2	Dimensions of Absorptive Capacity	83
7.3	Types of Innovation	84
7.4	Theoretical Framework	85
7.5	Behavioural HC-led Innovation Framework	87
9.1	Conceptual Framework	116
10.1	HC4.0 Hierarchy	139
10.2	Dimensions of HC4.0	140
10.3	Cognitive Abilities	141
10.4	Digital Skills	142
10.5	Emotional Skills	143
10.6	Attitudinal skills	144
10.7	Relative Importance of HC4.0	146

Tables

1.1	Selected Definitions of Human Capital	4
3.1	Experts Demography	28
4.1	Experts Demography	46
4.2	The Findings of AHP	46
6.1	Dimensions of Complexity of Task Environment	70
6.2	Enabling States for Human Capital Resource	71
7.1	Dimensions of Attitude	82
7.2	Dimensions of Personal Attributes	83
7.3	Respondent Firms Demography	88
7.4	Respondent Employees Demography	89
7.5	Sources of Constructs and their Indicators	89
7.6	Constructs Reliability and Vailidty	90
7.7	Fornell-Larcker Criteria	92
7.8	Path Analysis	93
7.9	Hypotheses Testing	93
9.1	Constructs and their Sources	119
9.2	Respondent Firms Demography	120
9.3	Respondents Employees demography	120
9.4	Reliability and Validity Statistics	121
9.5	Fornell-Larcker Criteria	122
9.6	Collinarity Statistics (VIF Value)	122
9.7	Path Analysis	123
10.1	Summary of Human Capital 4.0	144
10.2	Relative Prioritization of Human Capital 4.0 Dimensions and Sub-dimensions	145

Author Biographies

Dr. Muhammad Shahbaz is Professor (Tenured) of Energy Economics, School of Management and Economics, Beijing Institute of Technology, Beijing, China. Dr. Muhammad Shahbaz is Visiting Research Fellow at the Department of Land Economy, University of Cambridge. He is also Adjunct Professor at COMSATS University Islamabad, Lahore Campus, Lahore, Pakistan. He was the Chair Professor at Energy and Sustainable Development, Montpellier Business School France. He received his PhD in Economics from National College of Business Administration and Economics, Lahore Campus, Pakistan. His research focuses on development economics, energy economics, environmental and tourism economics, etc. He has widely published in peer-reviewed international journals. He has published more than 500 research papers so far in the national and international referred publications, having a cumulative impact factor of 1000 so far. With citations of 43247, he is ranked among the top three energy economists of the world. He has also been conferred the award of "Scientist of the Year Award" by the Turkish government. Dr. Shahbaz's area of interest is energy economics, environmental economics, and sustainability.

Prof. Dr. Muhammad Shujaat Mubarik is a Professor and Dean College of Business Management (CBM), IoBM, Karachi. His areas of interest are intellectual capital, supply chain management, and sustainability economics. He has more than 80 research papers (ISI/ABDC/AJG/Scopus indexed), published in journals of high repute, including *International Journal of Production Research, Technological Forecasting and Social Change, Business Strategy and Environment, Journal of Cleaner Production, Journal of Intellectual Capital, and Management Decision*. He has Springer's book *Dynamics of Intellectual Capital in Current Era* to his credit, which is the only handbook that covers IC from South Asian perspective. Dr. Mubarik has also contributed various book chapters in the international best-selling handbooks; prominent among them are *The Palgrave Handbook on Cross-Cultural Negotiation* and *The Palgrave Handbook of Corporate Sustainability in the Digital Era*. He has been the PI and Co-PI of various nationally and xiv *Author Biographies*

internationally funded projects. Presently, he is working on a funded project exploring the possible implementation of the blockchain-driven supply chain in Oil and Gas sector of Pakistan. Dr. Mubarik regularly appears in TV shows to share his opinion on national and international economics and business affairs. He can be reached at shujaat.mubarik@iobm.edu.pk.

Dr. Qaisar Abbas acquired a PhD degree in Human Resource Development from the Nankai University Tianjin, the PRC, in May 2000. He undertook post-doctoral research at Cardiff Business School (United Kingdom) in September 2007. He also holds MSc and MPhil in Economics from the Quaid-i-Azam University of Islamabad. He has worked as Dean of the Faculty of Business Administration at Comsats University Islamabad (CUI) and Director of CUI Lahore campus. Over the years, he has assumed various responsibilities at CUI, including Provost, Convener of Campus Selection Committee, Convener Board of Studies of Management Sciences, and Convener Board of Faculties of Business Administration and Board Member of Governor CUI in Pakistan.

Foreword

Today's modern world is in constant flux. We continue to accelerate from the old to the new paradigm at the speed of light. The new economy forces us to digitally transform, constantly pivot, and absorb new knowledge in an effort to create inimitable competitive advantage. At the core of this challenge is the critical role that human capital plays. Without it, our organizations are empty shells. Human capital is the critical resource that sustains our organizations and allows them to maintain their competitiveness. The academic discipline on human capital has a long and rich history. Human capital research started in the 1950s with influential economists such as Theodore Schultz, Garry Becker, and Jacob Mincer. Since then, human capital has remained one of the most vital areas of research, especially for academics in the fields of business and economics. Beyond academic research, the importance of human capital has also infiltrated the attention of senior managers and government policy makers. Indeed, human capital is among the most critical resources necessary for success at both the firm and national levels of analysis making it a bountiful concept for study in today's burgeoning marketplace.

By the mid-1990s, the field of intellectual capital had gained worldwide attention. Stock market analysts focused on the importance of intangible value as the main driver for economic success. This was especially true for technology-based organizations who realized valuations that were way beyond the means of their traditional physical assets. Analysts who followed companies such as Microsoft and Apple were assigning enormous value to their human capital assets which went beyond the extant accounting and financial models of the time. Human capital seemed to be at the core of such valuations and a new management phenomenon took off. In fact, human capital was deemed to become the antecedent for several important management initiatives at the time including organizational innovation, productivity, and learning.

This book, penned by Mubarik, Shahbaz, and Abbas, focuses on this important phenomenon. I have collaborated with Dr. Shujaat Mubarik and we have published several research studies together. Much of our work together is contained in this text. It gives me immense pleasure to see that our work in the field of human capital can be further shared with students, managers, researchers, and policymakers alike. The text is timely as we recover from the global effects of the COVID-19 pandemic. Moving forward, the importance placed on human capital as a driver for performance will be even greater. I encourage you all to enjoy the content of this book and embrace the concepts therein. Most importantly, I hope you continue to share and collaborate with others so that the lessons of effective human capital management can allow us to prosper for years to come.

Dr. Nick Bontis, PhD
www.NickBontis.com
Chair, Strategic Management
DeGroote School of Business
McMaster University
Hamilton, Ontario, Canada

Preface

The future as it is unfolding would be heavily virtual driven by artificial intelligence. Although the world of tomorrow has not yet unfolded itself completely, our preparation for its challenges is not sufficient. The glimpse of our inability was exposed by the COVID-19 pandemic. The world went through perilous times somewhat rescued by virtual connectivity. Human capital acts as the foundation of this new economy. The changing roles of human capital and social development have led to the necessity of a new paradigm of economic growth. In the new economic context, characterized by catastrophic pandemics and competitive pressures, human capital turns out to be an essential pillar of the economy that leads to the economic growth and development of a nation. At the firm level, besides directly contributing to the competitive advantage, an organization's human capital can be instrumental in attaining a balance between organizational efforts of exploitation and exploration and organizational ambidexterity. The majority of the organization, in the pursuit of existing business opportunities, ignores exploration. Whereas, in reality, central to the ability of a firm to survive over time is its ability to exploit existing assets and positions in a profit-producing way and simultaneously to explore new technologies and markets. Strong human capital has the potential to improve organizational competitiveness by making it an ambidextrous organization; however, thirst-quenching scholastic work is missing in this conception.

Similarly, less scholastic work has been steered in elucidating the role of ambidexterity in human capital-competitive advantage relationship, requiring researchers' attention. Further, given the influx of disruptive technologies and emphasize sustainability, some might ask as to how human capital would be perceived, measured, and transpired. Further, some may question the association of human capital with developments like big data, blockchain technologies, digital technologies, etc.

To answer these burning questions, we decided to come up with a book, catering the concept of human capital in greater diversity, written in a simple language, and offering practical strategies for human capital management and development. While writing this book, rather than solely relying upon literature analysis or empirical surveys, we took the opinions of number of HR experts across the globe, to keep the book xviii *Preface*

globally acceptable. Further, instead of offering a definite conclusion, each chapter of the book has been concluded with the concluding remarks, leaving the conclusion on the readers. We have also pointed out few potential areas of research in the last section of each chapter for the future researchers.

Muhammad Shahbaz, Muhammad Shujaat Mubarik, Qaisar Abbas

Acknowledgement

No effort, what-so-ever, can come to fruitful conclusion without the support of others. This book is no exception. There are people and organizations that need to be thanked for their support, guidance, and valuable inputs. First of all, I would thank, Dr. Muhammad Mumtaz Khan, who readily made himself available to give his input when required. We also extend our gratitude to Higher Education Commission (HEC) Pakistan for their support in data collection (under NRPU#20-11226) for the few chapters of the book. Finally, heartfelt thanks to Mr. Talib Syed Karim (President IoBM, Karachi) and Ms. Sabina Mohsin (Executive Director Administration IoBM Karachi), who always encourage to undertake the scholastic work that can benefit the country and society at large.

1 Human Capital: Evolution and Dimensions

1.1 Introduction

The turbulent economic environment, the influx of disruptive technologies, and the catastrophes of the COVID-19 have staggeringly disruptive impacts on the business landscape. These disruptions have reinforced what we already know: that human capital plays a crucial role not only in economic growth but also in fighting against crisis, disruptions, and chaos. In contrast to the other crisis, e.g., financial crisis, the COVID-19 pandemic is a humanitarian crisis at its core. Hence, human capital strategist, policy makers, and leaders have remained the centre of attention in the organizations to respond to this disruption. Further, given the present socio-economic scenarios, understanding the multi-facet roles of human capital has become ever important. Especially, the role of human capital in the context of technological development, innovation, resilience, and ambidextrous behaviour needs to be studied at priority. As noted by World Bank Report (2020, xii), "[human capital] requires serious attention given the severe impact of the pandemic on health and education. They further argue, "Boosting investment in human capital and climate resilience will be crucial to raise living standards and foster inclusive and sustainable growth" (World Bank Report 2020, p. vii).

Before proceeding as to how human capital can influence the pace of growth and performance at micro, meso, and macro levels, it is important to understand "as to what do we mean by human capital?" This conceptual clarity is important in order to examine the multifaced role of human capital and to develop the policies thereon. This chapter is devoted to exploring the evolution of human capital and its various definitions and dimensions. This chapter paves the way for the subsequent chapters as the definitions concluded in this chapter have been followed in the rest of the book.

1.2 Evolution of Human Capital

Although the concept of human capital could be traced back to the 18th-century economists (e.g., Adam Smith, John Stuart Mill, and Alfred) who

DOI: 10.4324/9781003195894-1

2 Human Capital: Evolution and Dimensions

highlighted the significance of the labours' ability in the productivity differences (Mubarik 2015; Sweetland 1996), the use of the term *human capital* to exhibit the economic contribution of training, health, and education of human beings was used by the late-50s economists. Most of the pre-WWII economic literature confined the role of education—the basic premise of human capital—at the social, moral, and political level and seldom considered its economic role (Teixeira 2014).

The post-WWII era showed an increase in the understanding and familiarity with the concept of human capital. Some economists between 1940 and 1955 tend to weigh the importance of education to generate economic value. For example, Frank Knight (1941) made human capital as the point of his research while discussing economic freedom (Teixeira 2014). Likewise, Milton Friedman also used the term human capital while discussing the postwar fiscal policy and personnel income distribution in his work (Friedman 1943; 1953). Notable among them is Allan fisher, who explicitly argued on the economic contribution of education and emphasized the role of education to generate economic value (Fisher AGB 1946). He held human skills scarcity responsible for hiccups in the economic system. Likewise, Roy Harrod made the human capital point of his discussion while explaining the reasons of unemployment (Harrod 1943; Teixeira 2014). Other notable economists who explicitly discussed human capital's concept include Kenneth Boulding and Joseph Spengler (Spengler 1950; 1955).

In the mid-50s, a group of economists from the department of economics, Chicago University, took the concept of human capital to the next level. The concept came under limelight when Theodore Schultz, the then Head of the Department of Economics, in his presidential address to the American Economic Society (AES), discussed as to why the human capital must be given importance and why the notion human capital was neither socially nor ethically wrong (Schultz 1961). Schultz (1961) challenged the conventional sociological and economic wisdom of not labelling humans as capital and negated any moral, ethical, or practical reason for not using the word capital for the human being. He argued, "[by using capital for human] laborers have become capitalists not from a diffusion of the ownership of corporation stocks, as folklore would have it, but from the acquisition of knowledge and skill that have economic value" (Schultz 1961, p. 3). He mentioned that technically advanced countries' superiority could be significantly attributed to the deliberate investments made in harnessing the knowledge, skills, and abilities of their population. For Schultz (1961), knowledge, skills, and abilities of human beings are the human capital that could be increased through investment in education, health, and training.

Beside Schultz, during 1950s, Edith Penrose and Jacob Mincer (1957) also put forward the importance of human capital. Penrose (1959) highlighted that human capital (managerial capabilities of managers) was responsible for the slow growth of an organization. This managerial constraint on the firm's growth rate is famously known as Penrose Effect. Mincer

(1957), denoting the significance of human capital in the economic process, mentioned education and training as the main reasons for income disparity among individuals.

1.3 Human Capital: Definitions and Dimensions

Since human capital equally matters for both individual firms and economies, it is essential to delineate it at the micro and macro levels.

The imprints of human capital could be found in the writings of Adam Smith, who considered the people as the most significant source of the wealth of a nation (Smith 1937); and Farr (1853), who measured the human capital net-worth of England, terming it as an essential component of growth. The work of these philosopher-cum-economists was expanded by the 50s economist who not only defined as to what human capital was but also provided scientific evidence on the role of human capital at the micro and macro levels. Mincer (1957), Schultz (1961), and Becker (1962) were the earlier economists who broadly explained the concept of human capital at macro level, defining HC as the knowledge, skills, and abilities (KSA) of the people that could be used to generate the economic value. As the concept of human capital gained popularity, its various dimensions were identified and analyzed by the researchers. For example, Nakamura (1981) added an individual's managerial, innovative, and entrepreneurial skills along with his/her health as the two essential dimensions of human capital. Following excerpts from Mubarik(2015) is important to understand the evlution of human capital during the 80s:

> Although the axiom of Chicago school economists caught the immediate attention of scholars to work on human capital, it was only in the late 80s when work on it captured the great interest of not only researchers and academia but also of the industry. One eminent reason was a rising competition in the markets and the success of the companies due to the abilities of their human capital. It was an era when businesses started realizing how the skills, abilities, attitudes, education and training of human capital could bring a difference. This rise in popularity resulted in a good scholastic contribution to the field of human capital. Many scholars, therefore, presented innovative dimensions and measures of human capital.

The aforementioned point could be one of the reasons for a variety of definitions and dimensions of human capital during the 90s. Table 1.1 exhibits a few selected definitions of human capital.

A brief review of literature also reveals that indicators such as education, entrepreneurial experience training, skills, related industry experience, organizational tenure, satisfaction, engagement commitment, emotional intelligence, stability, attitude, personal attributes, work-related competencies, health, innovation, social status, humanism, spiritualism, problem-solving abilities, and behaviour are the major HC indicators.

4 *Human Capital: Evolution and Dimensions*

Table 1.1 Selected Definitions of Human Capital

Definitions	Source(s)
The implicit or tacit knowledge of employees of a firm is its human capital.	Winter and Nelson (1982)
Human capital includes education, training, medical care, and other additions to knowledge and health [...] accumulated work and other habits, even including harmful addictions such as smoking and drug use.	Becker (1992), Nobel Prize Lecture
Employees' knowledge, experience, competence, and creativity are the important dimensions of human capital.	Brooking and Motta (1996)
Employee sustainability, satisfaction, and capability are important constituents of HC.	Kaplan and Norton (1996)
Knowledge (education), abilities, skills, and health are essential cords of human capital.	Becker et al. (1997)
Education and relevant industry cum work experience represent the human capital of an employee.	Gimeno et al. (1997)
Employees' attitudes, skills, and training form human capital.	Booth (1998)
Accumulation of talent and skills is human capital.	Mathur (1999)
It is the competence of employees attained through education.	Blundell et al. (1999)
Human capital differs at the micro and macro levels. At the micro level, HC represents an individual's education, abilities, and efforts, whereas at the macro level, it refers to as technological and institutional structures of an economy.	Dagum and Slottje (2000)
Accumulation of employees' skills, professional knowledge, expertise, and competence is HC.	Dzinkowski (2000)
HC represents the investment in people through education, training, retraining, skilling, and reskilling.	Pearce (2001)
Aggregation of employees' ability to perform assigned tasks, creativity, skills, and knowledge is HC.	Bontis (2001)
A fusion of factors such as education, experience, training, intelligence, energy, work habits, trustworthiness, and initiative that affect the value of a worker's marginal product.	Frank et al. (2007, p. 28)
Employees' education, personal experience, knowledge, professional skills, and innovative ability are the major strands of human capital.	Luthans et al. (2004)

(Continued)

Table 1.1 (Continued)

Definitions	Source(s)
Human capital is the fusion of technical, foundational, entrepreneurial, interpersonal, and 21st-century skills.	ILO (2008)
Education levels, skills like problem-solving, commitment, education, and training are major dimensions of HC.	Hatch and Dyer (2004)
Education, creativity, skills, and experience are important human capital factors.	Subramaniam and Youndt (2005)
Employees' organizational/professional tenure, commitment, and co-operativeness are the major indicators of HC.	Han et al. (2008)
Human capital constitutes the innate abilities of an individual, attained through education, skills achieved through training, and other pre-labour market influences.	Conley (2012)
HC is formed by a nation's health, skills, abilities, knowledge levels, innovations, humanism, culture, and spiritualism.	Alexandru and Maria (2012)
Along with education and experience, employees' work-related competencies and satisfaction are important HC indicators.	Rompho and Siengthai (2012)
Human capital represents knowledge, training, skills, abilities, attitudes, attributes, health, compliance, and stability of employees of an organization.	Mubarik (2015)
The stock of abilities and skills possessed by labour force.	Pasban and Nojedeh (2016)
Human capital comprises of three important dimensions of employees of a firm. These dimensions are qualification, satisfaction and creativity, and leadership and motivation.	Vidotto et al. (2017); Mahmood and Mubarik (2020); Mubarik and Naghavi(2020)
Human capital can be categorized into general and specific aspects. The general human capital is shaped by education, health, etc., whereas specific human capital is formed by way of training (e.g, OJTs, technical training, and experience.	Flabbi and Gatti (2018)
Firm-level human capital comprises of acumen developed through training, skills, extrinsic, and education. It also considers the interpersonal relationships of employees.	Hsu and Chen (2019); Ahmad et al. (2019)
Employees' education, experience, and age are the major indicators of a firm's human capital and can significantly influence its innovation performance.	Sun et al. (2020); Khan at al. (2020)
HC represents the resources linked with individuals' skills, abilities, and knowledge.	Angrist et al. (2021); Chamadia and Mubarik (2021); Mubarik et al. (2021)

(Continued)

6   Human Capital: Evolution and Dimensions

Table 1.1 (Continued)

Definitions	Source(s)
HC is the intrinsic motivation, abilities, personality traits, and behaviour of individuals as well as their mental, physical, and emotional health, which can be employees for gaining economic benefits social and personal well-being.	Mubarik (2015; 2016); Mubarik et al. (2018); UNECE (2016); Mendoza et al. (2022)

1.4 Human Capital Theory

The award of five Nobel prizes—*Theodore W. Schultz 1979; Gary S. Becker 1992; Milton Friedman 1976; Simon Kuznets 1971; Robert M. Solow 1987*—to the scholars directly or indirectly related to the field of human capital theory bespoke its importance (Sweetland 1996). The basic premise of the HCT was the capitalization of human knowledge, skills, and abilities for the individual and societal economic benefits. Despite the notable work of other economists on human capital, it was Garry Becker, a student of Theodre Schultz and Chicago school professor, who provided the theoretical foundation to the concept of human capital by offering human capital theory (Becker 1962). Becker (1962) argued that anything contributing to the humans skills and abilities provide a long-term return and should be considered as investment. In doing so, he differentiated the normal expenditures from the expenditures made on education, health, and training, etc.–investment on human capital (Becker 1962; Mubarik 2015; Sweetland 1996). Becker (1962, p. 9) explains investment in human capital as, "the many ways to invest include schooling, on-the-job training, medical care, vitamin consumption, and acquiring information about the economic system." Human capital warranted special focus to the education, health, and training and put them forward as the major constituents of human capital. For HCT, human capital is output of the deliberate investment in the education, health, and training. Becker (1962) argues that efforts and fund spent on the improving the education, skills, and abilities of the labour force are investment expenditure, which give higher return in future. In nutshell, *cetrius peribus*, the basic premise of the HCT is that human capital in the shape of education, experience, training, and health is responsible for the productivity difference in the individuals and firms.

Some of the economists differ with the HCT and refute the claim of that human capital has a direct influence on productivity. For example, Richard Freeman, in 1976, argued that HC only is an indication of the level of talent an organization possesses; however, it does not guarantee the increase in productivity. The productivity difference comes from the training, development, motivation, and management of human capital along with the right type of capital equipment and machinery. Based on his argument, he refuted the role of human capital as the factor of production. Likewise, Gintis and Samuel Bowels, two famous Marxist economists, rejected the notion "human capital" claiming humans can't be commodified. They further argued that turning the human (labour) into capital can create serious moral issues and trigger class conflicts. Recent studies in the field of economics mention that the human capital theory oversimplifies the HC and productivity association.

1.5 Concluding Remarks

Since this chapter sets the stage for the rest of the book, it is essential to discuss some fundamental conceptual differences in understating human capital. The roots of human capital can be traced back to the 18th century when the economists Adam Smith and Alfred Marshal highlighted the labours quantitative and qualitative inputs as the basis of productivity. Nevertheless, the exhausting literature review reveals that theorization and substantiation of the human capital concept could be traced back to Professor Theodore Schultz and Garry Becker. These economists explicitly mentioned education, training, and health as the major constituents of human capital, and these explain the difference in the individual's income. Later on, this definition was expanded by various researchers, practitioners, and institutions, adding aspects like behaviour, emotional intelligence, dexterity, personality traits, motivation, judgment, and other aspects that can contribute to the economic value creation social and personal well-being. Interestingly, researchers from endogenous growth theories and neoclassical schools of thought both recognize the instrumental role of human capital and consider human capital development essential for performance at micro, meso, and macro levels. Given the present scenario, where rapidly changing international socio–political events and COVID-19 have drastically affected businesses globally, it is essential to understand the determinants, strategies, and approaches to increase human capital accumulation and development levels. Further, despite the fact that the role of human capital is recognized, it is essential to explain how it matters for modern-day performance parameters like organizational ambidexterity, internalization, innovation, and technological adoption.

Against this backdrop, this book partly contributes to the aforementioned debate by explicitly exploring four essential dimensions of human capital. First, how human capital could be measured and what could be the most appropriate approach in this respect. Second, what could be the strategies, approaches, and practices that can help the firm to better capitalize on its existing stock of human capital. Third, what are the important human capital traits and dimensions in the context of contemporary market dynamics like the post–COVID-19 scenario, the influx of Industry 4.0 driven technologies, and internationalization. Fourth, as to how HC can uplift the organizational ambidexterity, internalization, innovation, and technological

8 *Human Capital: Evolution and Dimensions*

adoption. In doing so, this book contributes to the contemporary debate on the role and type of human capital at the micro and macro levels and helps understand the strategies for HC measurement, development, and employment.

Before ending this chapter, it is essential to explain our views on the ongoing debate on HC and human capital resources (HCR) difference. The term human capital represents individual employees' knowledge, skills, and abilities, whereas human capital resource (HCR) represents the aggregate firm-level KSA organization. For Polyhart and Moliterno (2011, p. 128), "[human capital is] unit-level resource that is created from the emergence of individuals' knowledge, skills, abilities, and other characteristics (KSAOs)." They further argue, "the collective unit-level human capital resource originates in individual-level employee KSAO" (p. 128). Some of the studies (e.g., Aryee et al., 2016) have also termed it collective human capital, which illustrates the collective ability of an organization to perform any task. We have used HC and HCR interchangeably throughout this book. Nonetheless, we suggest future researchers explore how HC and HCR could differentiate.

References

Ahmed, S. S., Guozhu, J., Mubarik, S., Khan, M., & Khan, E. (2019). Intellectual capital and business performance: the role of dimensions of absorptive capacity. *Journal of Intellectual Capital*, 21(1), 23–39.

Alexandru, J., & Maria, T. (2012). Dimensions of human capital–specific health approach of nations capital. *Annals of Faculty of Economics*, 1(1), 312–317.

Angrist, N., Djankov, S., Goldberg, P. K., & Patrinos, H. A. (2021). Measuring human capital using global learning data. *Nature*, 592(7854), 403–408.

Aryee, S., Walumbwa, F. O., Seidu, E. Y., & Otaye, L. E. (2016). Developing and leveraging human capital resource to promote service quality: Testing a theory of performance. *Journal of management*, 42(2), 480–499.

Becker, G. S. (1962). Investment in human capital: A theoretical analysis. *Journal of political economy*, 70(5, Part 2), 9–49.

Becker, G. S. (1992). The economic way of looking at life. Accessed from: https://chicagounbound.uchicago.edu/cgi/viewcontent.cgi?article=1509&context=law_and_economics

Becker, B. E., Huselid, M. A., Pickus, P. S., & Spratt, M. F. (1997). HR as a source of shareholder value: Research and recommendations. *Human Resource Management*, 36(1), 39–47.

Blundell, R., Dearden, L., Meghir, C., & Sianesi, B. (1999). Human capital investment: the returns from education and training to the individual, the firm and the economy. *Fiscal Studies*, 20(1), 1–23.

Bontis, N. (1998). Intellectual capital: An exploratory study that develops measures and models. *Management Decision*, 36(2), 63–76.

Bontis, N. (2001). Assessing knowledge assets: A review of the models used to measure intellectual capital. *International Journal of Management Reviews*, 3(1), 41–60.

Booth, R. (1998). The measurement of intellectual capital. *Management Accounting (UK)*, 76(1), 26–28.

Brooking, A., & Motta, E. (1996). A taxonomy of intellectual capital and a methodology for auditing it. 17th Annual National Business Conference, McMaster University, Hamilton, Ontario.

Chamadia, S., & Mubarik, M. S. (2021). Assessing the effectiveness of vocational training programs in Pakistan: An experimental study. *Education+ Training*, 63(5), 665–678.

Conley, D. M. (2012). Cultural dimensions of human capital development. *International Food and Agribusiness Management Review*, 15(1), 44–68.

Dagum, C., & Slottje, D. J. (2000). A new method to estimate the level and distribution of household human capital with application. *Structural Change and Economic Dynamics*, 11(1), 67–94.

Diebolt, C., & Hippe, R. (2022). The long-run impact of human capital on innovation and economic growth in the regions of Europe. In *Human Capital and Regional Development in Europe* (pp. 85–115). Springer, Cham.

Dzinkowski, R. (2000). The measurement and management of intellectual capital: An introduction. *Management Accounting*, 78(2), 32–36.

Farr, W. (1853). The income and property tax. *Journal of the Statistical Society of London*, 16(1), 1–44.

Fisher AGB (1946). *Education and Economic Change*. W. E. A. Press, South Australia.

Flabbi, L. and Gatti, R. A. (January 19, 2018). Primer on Human Capital. World Bank Policy Research Working Paper No. 8309, Available at SSRN: https://ssrn.com/abstract=3105769

Frank, R. H., Bernanke, B., & Johnston, L. D. (2007). *Principles of Economics*. McGraw-Hill/Irwin, New York

Friedman, M. (1943). The spendings tax as a wartime fiscal measure. *The American Economic Review*, 33(1), 50–62.

Friedman, M. (1953). Choice, chance, and the personal distribution of income. *Journal of Political Economy*, 61(4), 277–290.

Gimeno, J., Folta, T. B., Cooper, A. C., & Woo, C. Y. (1997). Survival of the fittest? Entrepreneurial human capital and the persistence of underperforming firms. *Administrative Science Quarterly*, 42(4), 750–783.

Goldin, Claudia (2016). Human capital. In *Handbook of Cliometrics*, ed. Claude Diebolt and Michael Haupert (pp. 55–86). Springer Verlag, Heidelberg, Germany.

Han, T.-S., Lin, C. Y.-Y., & Chen, M. Y.-C. (2008). Developing human capital indicators: A threeway approach. *International Journal of Learning and Intellectual Capital*, 5(3), 387–403.

Harrod, R. F. (1943). Full employment and security of livelihood. *The Economic Journal*, 53(212), 321–342.

Hatch, N. W., & Dyer, J. H. (2004). Human capital and learning as a source of sustainable competitive advantage. *Strategic Management Journal*, 25(12), 1155–1178.

Hsu, B. X., & Chen, Y. M. (2019). Industrial policy, social capital, human capital, and firm-level competitive advantage. *International Entrepreneurship and Management Journal*, 15(3), 883–903.

International Labour Organization. (2008). *Issues in workplace learning in Asia and the Pacific*. ILO, Genève, Switzerland. Retrieved from: http://www.ilo.org/wcmsp5/groups/public/---asia/---robangkok/documents/publication/wcms_098875.pdf (Accessed: January 02, 2015).

Jones, B. F. (2019). The human capital stock: A generalized approach: reply. *American Economic Review*, 109(3), 1175–1195.

10 *Human Capital: Evolution and Dimensions*

Kaplan, R. S., & Norton, D. P. (1996). Using the balanced scorecard as a strategic management system. *Harvard Business Review*, 74(1), 75–85.

Khan, M. M., Mubarik, M. S., Ahmed, S. S., Islam, T., Khan, E., Rehman, A., & Sohail, F. (2021). My meaning is my engagement: exploring the mediating role of meaning between servant leadership and work engagement. *Leadership & Organization Development Journal*, 42(6), 926–941.

Knight, F. H. (1941). The role of the individual in the economic world of the future. *Journal of Political Economy*, 49(6), 817–832.

Luthans, F., Luthans, K. W., & Luthans, B. C. (2004). Positive psychological capital: Beyond human and social capital. *Business Horizons*, 47(1), 45–50.

Mahmood, T., & Mubarik, M. S. (2020). Balancing innovation and exploitation in the fourth industrial revolution: Role of intellectual capital and technology absorptive capacity. *Technological Forecasting and Social Change*, 160, 120248.

Mathur, V. K. (1999). Human capital-based strategy for regional economic development. *Economic Development Quarterly*, 13(3), 203–216.

Mendoza, O. M. V., Borsi, M. T., & Comim, F. (2022). Human capital dynamics in China: Evidence from a club convergence approach. *Journal of Asian Economics*, 101441.

Mincer, J. (1957). *A Study of Personal Income Distribution*. Columbia University.

Mubarik, M. S. (2015). *Human capital and performance of small & medium manufacturing enterprises: A study of Pakistan* (Doctoral dissertation, University of Malaya). Accessed from: https://core.ac.uk/download/pdf/268878007.pdf (February 2020).

Mubarik, M. S., Govindaraju, C., & Devadason, E. S. (2016). Human capital development for SMEs in Pakistan: Is the "one-size-fits-all" policy adequate? *International Journal of Social Economics*. 43(8), 804–822.

Mubarik, M. S., Chandran, V. G. R., & Devadason, E. S. (2018). Measuring human capital in small and medium manufacturing enterprises: What matters? *Social Indicators Research*, 137(2), 605–623.

Mubarik, M. S., Devadason, E. S., & Govindaraju, C. (2020). Human capital and export performance of small and medium enterprises in Pakistan. *International Journal of Social Economics*, 47(5), 643–662.

Mubarik, M. S., & Naghavi, N. (2020). Human capital, green energy, and technological innovations: Firm-level analysis. In *Econometrics of Green Energy Handbook* (pp. 151–164). Springer, Cham.

Mubarik, M. S., Bontis, N., Mubarik, M., & Mahmood, T. (2021). Intellectual capital and supply chain resilience. *Journal of Intellectual Capital*. Ahead of print. 10.1108/JIC-06-2020-0206

Nakamura, J. I. (1981). Human capital accumulation in premodern rural Japan. *The Journal of Economic History*, 41(2), 263–281.

Pasban, M., & Nojedeh, S. H. (2016). A review of the role of human capital in the organization. *Procedia-social and behavioral sciences*, 230, 249–253.

Pearce, R. (2001). Multinationals and industrialisation: The bases of 'inward investment'policy. *International Journal of the Economics of Business*, 8(1), 51–73.

Penrose, E. T. (1959). *The Theory of the Growth of the Firm*. JohnWiley, New York.

Rompho, B., & Siengthai, S. (2012). Integrated performance measurement system for firm's human capital building. *Journal of Intellectual Capital*, 13(4), 482–514.

Schultz, T. W. (1961). Investment in human capital. *The American economic review*, 51(1), 1–17.

Smith, A. (1937). *The Wealth of Nations [1776] Carman Edition*. Modern Library, New York.

Spengler, J. J. (1950). Some economic aspects of the subsidization by the state of the formation of "human capital". *Kyklos*, 4(4), 316–342.

Spengler, J. J. (1955). Socioeconomic theory and population policy. *American Journal of Sociology*, 61(2), 129–133.

Subramaniam, M., & Youndt, M. A. (2005). The influence of intellectual capital on the types of innovative capabilities. *Academy of Management Journal*, 48(3), 450–463.

Sweetland, S. R. (1996). Human capital theory: Foundations of a field of inquiry. *Review of educational research*, 66(3), 341–359.

Sun, X., Li, H., & Ghosal, V. (2020). Firm-level human capital and innovation: Evidence from China. *China Economic Review*, 59, 101388.

Teixeira, P. N. (2014). Gary Becker's early work on human capital–collaborations and distinctiveness. *IZA Journal of Labor Economics*, 3(1), 1–20.

United Nations. Economic Commission for Europe. (2016). *Guide on measuring human capital*. UN.

Vidotto, J. D. F., Ferenhof, H. A., Selig, P. M., & Bastos, R. C. (2017). A human capital measurement scale. *Journal of Intellectual Capital*, 18(2), 316–329.

Winter, S. G., & Nelson, R. R. (1982). An evolutionary theory of economic change. *University of Illinois at Urbana-Champaign's Academy for Entrepreneurial Leadership Historical Research Reference in Entrepreneurship*. Available at SSRN: http://ssrn.com/abstract=1496211

World Bank Report (2020). COVID19 and Human Capital. *World Bank Group: Europe and Central Asia Economic Update*. Accessed from: https://openknowledge.worldbank.org/bitstream/handle/10986/34518/9781464816437.pdf (January 2022).

2 Human Capital: Gauging the Ungauged

2.1 Introduction

Human capital comprises employees' knowledge, experience, and skills and their motivation and willingness to employ these traits to create value. It implies that gauging levels of human capital is not merely a measurement of employees' skills and knowledge; it is also important to how effectively these KSAs could be employed to contribute economic value for the organization. As noted by Lepak and Snell (1999), the real value of a firm's human capital depends upon its potential to create organizational value and contribute to organizational core competencies. Many human capital measures are available, claiming to capture the true level of human capital in a firm; still, there is no consensus on any comprehensive measure of it (Mubarik et al. 2018). Perhaps, one of the major reasons could be the context specificity of the human capital measures, as noted by Baron (2011). Likewise, an HC measure that can precisely gauge the C levels today may not be relevant tomorrow due to the rapidly changing dynamics. It reflects that HC measurement is an evolving process. This is why organizations keep constantly reviewing, upgrading, and developing the measure of HC to better align with the contemporary rules of the games.

There are certainly some other important reasons to measure human capital at the organizational level. First, since human capital is linked to employees and is likely to put exigent management control issues, its measurement is essential (Widener 2004). Second, human capital measurement is vital in strategic decisions like formulating business strategies or taking expansion decisions. Third, a company needs to measure its level of human capital to analyze the organizational effectiveness and to communicate with investors. Besides it, at the policy level, it is important to know how the level of HC differs from various perspectives, particularly differences in human capital by industry, size, and ownership can be an important input for policymaking.

Against the aforementioned backdrop, this chapter briefly reviews various HC measures used at the micro and macro levels and offers insights to improve the precision and relevance of HC measure.

DOI: 10.4324/9781003195894-2

2.2 Measuring Human Capital: Methodological Approaches and Issues

2.2.1 Macro-measurement Methodologies

Methods to gauge human capital stock at the nation level fall into two major categories i.e., monetary-based approaches and indicator-based approaches.

A. Monetary-based Approaches
These approaches tend to quantify the contribution or value of human capital in monetary values. These approaches have two broader categories, i.e., cost-based approach and income-based approach. The following text explains each of the categories.

   I. Cost-based Approaches: Engel developed this approach to measure the national stock of human capital (Mubarik 2015). He estimated the value of human capital based on the cost incurred on rearing a human. The method, he explained, was that all of the expenditures incurred in order to rear a child up to the age of 25 would be counted as human capital. Since this approach was just a summation of the historical cost incurred on a person, this was its major snag (Dagum & Slottje 2000). Kendrick (1976) ameliorated this method by illustrating the tangible and intangible (tacit) aspect of human capital. The tangible part referred to expenditures needed to nurture physical human beings; whereas, the intangible part focused on expenses that enhanced productivity. Expenditures like those on health, education, training, and opportunity costs of students attending school were included to account for human capital. Eisner (1988) further calibrated this approach by allowing the inclusion of the value of a household's non-market activities in child-rearing.
   Though this approach is now a useful and easy measure, it has some drawbacks. First, it can estimate the human capital value over (or under). For example, there is a possibility that rearing a child who is dull or has some deficiency requires a larger amount of funds than what a normal child needs. Looking into the cost incurred, the human capital of a dull child is greater than that of a normal child. Yet, in reality, it is not. Secondly, it is challenging to bifurcate the investment from spending. It is hard to determine which part of household expenditure contributes to human capital and which does not. Thirdly, the marginal contribution of each investment spending is difficult to find. Lastly, Kendrick (1976) adopted the double-declining method, which depreciated human capital like physical capital. He adopted this method to keep it aligned with the depreciation of physical assets. Contradictorily, human capital can also appreciate with the passage of time (Dagum & Slottje 2000).

14 *Human Capital: Gauging the Ungauged*

II. Income-based Approach: In contrast to the cost-based approache, the income-based approach is forward-looking. It measures the future value of the human capital at the present time. For Rosen (1987, p. 682), "William Petty, the early actuary, and national income accountant is generally credited with the first serious application of the concept of human capital when in 1676 he compared the loss of armaments, machinery and other instruments of warfare with the loss of human life". Farr (1853) expanded this approach by taking human capital as the present value of a person's total future earnings minus their living expenses. Using a 5% discount rate, he calculated the present value of the future earning of an individual's net of living expenses and adjusted it for death expenses too. A number of earlier researchers (Barriol 1910; Nicholson 1891; Wittstein 1867) used this approach to measure human capital. However, Dublin and Lotka (1930) further improved this approach, which was productive and easy to use. Interestingly, the improved version had some serious flaws. First, it assumed that the wages of a person were paid based truly on his human capital contribution, which might not be the case in reality. Many exogenous factors can influence wages. For example, the pressure exerted by labor unions can result in high wages; or, in the case of unfavourable economic conditions, labour wages can decrease. Secondly, the availability of data on earnings, especially in the case of LDCs, was a severe issue.

Several researchers like Weisbrod (1961) and Graham and Webb (1979) revamped it to remove these flaws. Notably, Graham and Webb (1979) altered its structure to ingest economic growth. Further, Jorgenson and Fraumeni (1992) improved the method by simplifying the discounting future income flows to the present value (PV).

B. Indicator-based Approaches

The indicator-based approaches are generally based on the physical measures of human capital. Two types of approaches are prominently used, i.e., education indicator-based approaches and health indicator-based approaches. The following is a brief discussion of these approaches.

I. Education Indicators: In education, base human capital approaches are measured based on educational indicators like years of schooling, enrolment rate, literacy rate, and dropout rates. The rationale of using academic indicators for human capital is the notion that investment in education represents a significant portion of investment in human capital. The following are some major educational indicators used for human capital measurement.

a. Adult Literacy Rate (ALR): Adult literacy means the ability of a person above 15 years of age to read and write. Some researchers used this indicator to represent human capital. However, ALR has a minimal explanatory power and leaves many important elements like advanced knowledge and skills. Researchers mainly recommend using this in a country where the level of education is very low.

b. School Enrolment Rates (SER): School enrolment rates are gauged by dividing the total number of children who should attend school by the students enrolled at a given level. They are further divided into two categories, i.e., *gross enrolment rate and net enrolment rate*. The former takes the total number of students enrolled at a given level, whereas the latter excludes the students who do not belong to the designated age group. Barro et al. (1995) and Mankiw et al. (1992) used school enrolment rates to proxy for human capital. Researchers recommend taking primary enrolment rate for low-income countries, secondary enrolment rate for middle-income countries, and higher enrolment rate for rich countries as a proxy of human capital. Clarifying this phenomenon, Judson (2002) delineated a direct relationship of growth with human capital accumulation at the primary level for developing countries.

   School enrollment rate is taken as a proxy because it shows the flow that adds to the present stock of education to establish further stocks. This means it measures the present investment in human capital that will be reflected in the future. This is also a drawback on enrolment rates as a representative of human capital since there is a wide lag effect between enrolment rates and human capital addition. A student registering today will be part of a labour force several years later if they continue their education without any gap. Secondly, since it gauges the flow of stock that is part of accumulation, it does not encapsulate the total value of human capital.

c. Average Years of Schooling: Compared to enrolment rate and literacy ratio, the number of years of schooling is a better measure of human capital because it captures the investment on education in a better way. According to Le et al. (2005, p. 20) *"the studies that have attempted to develop data series on years of schooling can be conveniently divided into three group based on the method they employ: the census/survey-based estimation method, the projection method, and the perpetual inventory method"*. These scholars have captured the years of schooling more productively and realistically.

   With an adequate availability of data and better theoretical backing, the years of schooling measurement has been enormously employed in empirical researches on human capital. This is one of the common proxies being used at firm and nation level to represent the human capital. Despite these facts, it has some serious anomalies. The first irregularity observed is the inter-country and intra-country differences in the quality of education. The years of schooling method is incapable of observing these differences. Secondly, the years of schooling measurement is inept in capturing the difference in investment and a return on education at different levels. The years of schooling measurement assumes a constant return from each year of education, but it contradicts the empirical literature. Empirical studies have depicted decreasing returns to education (Psacharopoulos 1994). The third and most unrealistic assumption is the substitutability of workers. While taking years of schooling as a proxy, it is assumed that the labour of diverse education streams have the same type and quality of education.

Education-based approaches for gauging human capital are easy to enumerate and have copious international data. Nevertheless, these approaches have many serious gaps. The main critique is that they do not adequately present critical facets of human capital; this is especially so regarding the issue of quality which is ignored. This is why the use of these measures has resulted in contradictory results. For example, Mulligan and Sala-i-Martin (1997), using education as a proxy of human capital, found no relationship of human capital with economic growth.

To understand human capital better, the OECD developed an index based on different educational indicators. They took three significant dimensions of education, i.e., investment in education, quality adjustments, and results of education. Each dimension was sub-divided into different elements, encapsulating the multi-dimensional view of human capital.

II. Health Indicator-based Approaches: It is discernible that with any specified combination of capital (physical), technology, skills, and the improving health of employees, a firm can produce a higher amount of output. The poor health conditions give rise to absenteeism, low work motivation, and weak organizational commitments and drastically reduce the productivity level of a firm. At the macro level, economic development's goal remains unattainable without sustainable health conditions. Many scholars (e.g., Bloom et al. 2004; Lucas 1990; Qadri & Waheed 2011) used *health to represent* human capital. Among them, the self-reported health survey of population is considered the most appropriate. The resulting data were used to represent their health. The average life expectancy at birth is also deemed a prominent indicator. Moreover, indicators like years of potential life lost (YPLL), adult survival rate (ASR), and average life expectancy for men are also among the widely used indicators

(Mubarik 2015)). The incidence of obesity, arthritis, diabetes, cancer, accidents, and/and HIV/AIDS are also used as health indicators. The composite of these indicators are normally used to find health sustainability. Researchers have also used adult survival rates to represent health.

2.2.2 Micro-measurement Methodologies

Numerous researchers and management practitioners used various approaches to ascertain the human capital at the firm level. Major approaches to gauge human capital can be divided into five categories. Scholz et al. (2007) explained them, which has been presented in the following text.

A. Market Value Approaches

In market value approaches, companies measure their human capital based on the number of employees, their market values, and book value. Study of Fitz-Enz (2000) appears to be the most prolific in this category. He developed metrics to quantify the market value of human capital. Previously, Tobin (1969) adopted similar measures to compute human capital. Though these market value-based techniques quantify the different aspects of human capital well, they overlook some major qualitative facets of human capital. One of the major critique on this approach is that it narrowed down the human capital to a mere financial residual.

B. Accounting-oriented Approaches

Approaches in this category employ the accounting-related measures and methodologies to gauge the human capital measurement. Initially, Likert (1961) and Pyle (1966) attempted to use the accounting frameworks for developing an accounting measure of human capital investments. Flamholtz (1973), working on this, developed a comprehensive approach for gauging human capital. He took acquisition cost and learning cost as the two major dimensions of human capital cost. Acquisition cost is linked with the recruitment and selection, onboarding, deploying, and promoting a human resource. Whereas, the cost of formal training and on-the-job training (OJT) were included in the learning cost. His approach quantified both of these costs. This approach further emerged into a more-improved version when Flamholtz (1999) developed the stochastic rewards valuation model (SRVM) to value a firm's human capital. He developed a five-step method for human valuation to apply the SRVM. In the Flamholtz model framework, Flamholtz et al. (2003) also devised a practical approach to calculate ROI on management development and portrayed the marginal cash flows that a company would get due to investment in management development. To them, human resource accounting, which is a method to gauge the contribution of management development, augmented human capital value.

18 *Human Capital: Gauging the Ungauged*

Equally, Mirvis and Macy (1976) also measured human capital in an accounting frame. They incorporated human output (productivity) through behavioural variables. They divided behaviour into work participation behaviours and job performance behaviours. The cost of human capital was operationalized by taking outlay costs, time costs, fixed costs, variable costs, and opportunity costs. These costs reflected direct and indirect costs and lost-profit potential. Their results were robust, and they claimed their technique to be more valid, reliable, and valuable.

Other researchers also presented such an alternate model. For example, Cascio (1998) put forward dimensions like employee attitudes, human capital innovation, and the inventory of knowledgeable employees as a base to measure human capital. This approach gave innovation key importance. With regards to employees' attitudes as a predictor of customer satisfaction and retention, he emphasized the need to measure human capital. An employee's organizational tenure, turnover, experience, and learning were important inputs for human capital accounting.

The main accounting-oriented approaches view human capital as an investment account. Nevertheless, accounting base measurements of human capital are used in several organizations across the globe; researchers argue that there still is a need for fair value accounting (Bullen & Eyler, 2010).

C. Human Resource Indicator Approaches

A large clump of approaches used variables like experience, employee engagement, commitment, emotional quotient, motivation, knowledge, creativity, and skills to operationalize HC of a firm. For example, Gimeno et al. (1997) used experience and education to measure the level of human capital. Whereas, Bontis and Fitz-Enz (2002) took both qualitative and quantitative human capital factors to check the association between human capital effectiveness with human capital valuation, investment, and depletion. Following the methodology used by Saratoga Institute, they abstracted four factors, i.e., "revenue per full-time equivalent" (FTE), "expense per FTE", and human capital (ROI). They calculated these factors using the criteria developed by the Saratoga Institute. To demonstrate the applicability of their proposed method, Bontis and Fitz-Enz (2002) collected the data from both qualitative and quantitative measures. The data on revenue, full-time equivalents, compensation, training and development expenditure, voluntary and involuntary turnover, and employee separation rate was directly collected from companies under the study. They collected the data for qualitative measure through questionnaires. They also gathered the data on 15 human capital indicators. Their findings illustrated a direct association between HC effectiveness and organizational tenure of employees.

A few prominent techniques based on the indicators approach are Human Resources (HR) Scorecards (Stewart & Ruckdeschel 1998), Skandia Navigator (Edvinsson & Malone 1997), HR Scorecard (Becker et al. 1997), and Human Capital Indicator (Mohr & Keilholz 2001). Some

Human Capital: Gauging the Ungauged 19

of the researchers also used the Analytical Hierarchal Approach (AHP) for human capital calibration (Calabrese 2012; Calabrese et al. 2013).

D. Value-added Approaches

Value-added approaches are based on the difference between input and output. These approaches assume that the difference between input and output, and value addition, can be attributed to the human capital. Market value-added (MVA) and economic value-added approaches are the two most prominent approaches in the family of value-added approaches (Mubarik 2015; Young 1997).

I. EVA—Economic Value Added: It is regarded as an essential measure of corporate performance. EVA is calculated as follows:

$$EVA = (Cost\ of\ capital - return\ on\ capital)$$
$$\times\ the\ capital\ outstanding\ at\ the\ beginning\ of\ the\ year$$

It computes the difference between the return on a company's capital and its cost.

II. MVA—Market Value Added: It is the difference between a firm's market value and capital employed. It is measured as the value that a company has created above the resources already committed to the enterprise (Martin & Petty 2001). Harvey and Lusch (1997) used this technique to valuation intangible assets. It is worth mentioning that MVA approach cannot be used by companies who have publicly traded shares.

E. Market Return Approaches

The basic assumption behind market return approaches is "human capital is the major source of market return". The human capital pricing (HCP) model and the ROI of human capital (Bender & Röhling 2001). Saratoga Institute (Bontis et al. 1999) created the human capital financial index that combined the following three indexes: human capital revenue index, human capital cost index, and human capital profit index. Alhough this approach quantified the market return of human capital well, it ignored some of the vital issues. For example, the company's human capital was performing well, but due to external factors, its market value had reduced. In this case, the market return approach tended to undermine the value of human capital, but in the reverse situation, it would overvalue.

F. Other Approaches

Like the Sarotaga Institute, management practitioners developed specific analytical indexes to analyze human capital information. Some of the major indexes are discussed in brief as follows:

I. Balance Score Card: One of the famous indexes is the balanced score card. Initially, developed by Kaplan and Norton (1996), its tailored version is extensively used for human capital analysis. The unique aspect of the balanced scorecard is its systematic representation of multiple objectives as a basis for target setting. It considers HR issues equal to financial problems. Nonetheless, over-engineering of it can result in confusion and inconsistent results.

II. Human Capital Monitor: Mayo (2001) configured the human capital monitor to assess the worth of the human asset of a company. The main argument of Mayo (2001) is that people are assets, not cost. Human capital monitor focused on three issues. First, how could a company reveal the implicit diversity of its human resource and how could it be valued? Second, how could people's performance be logged into a metric? Third, how would one find the way to quantify effectively the monetary and non-monetary value to business stakeholders? Thus, Mayo introduced the individual asset multiplier (IAM), the weighted average of factors like HR performance, HR value alignment, HR capabilities, and the potential to grow. Its key benefit is the quantification of human capital in terms of monetary value. However, in order to use this model effectively, it rests on a company's ability to effectively calculate contribution and capabilities, etc. (Mayo 2012).

III. The Organizational Performance Model of Mercer HR Consulting: Developed in 1990 by Mercer Consulting, the model identified six key components that constituted a company's human capital strategy. These components were "people, work process, managerial structure, information and knowledge, decision-making and rewards" (Mubarik et al. 2018). The interconnectedness among these elements was a key to the organization's success.

IV. Human Capital Index: Mubarik et al. (2018) introduced the human capital index having 9 dimensions and 36 sub-dimensions of human capital. This index is comparatively comprehensive as it considers HC's qualitative and quantitative aspects. The index was built using expert's onion and by employing analytical hierarchal process (AHP). Nevertheless, too many dimensions and sub-dimensions make it complex to measure the level of human capital from various firms (Ahmed et al. 2019).

2.3 Concluding Remarks

As noted by Mubarik et al. (2018, p. 606), *"initial measures of HC seemed to focus solely on efficiency and cost. Traditional measures were highly criticized as they were considered short-term, lagging behind and backward-looking. This gave rise to the development of the HC metrics. This new concept urged organizations to apply non-financial performance measures for performance management such as the Balance Score Card and the Skandia's HC indicator"*. Thus, human capital measures emerge to gauge more than just efficiency measures with adapted measures for more complicated jobs (Gates 2004; Mubarik 2015). However, despite the approaches mentioned in the preceding section, there remain some major issues that need to be addressed regarding the effective measurement of human capital.

The problem with the traditional human capital approaches is that they focus on either the qualitative aspects of human capital such as attitude, satisfaction, or quantitative aspects like training expenses, labor costs, or revenues. For example, Scholz et al. (2007) mentioned that though market value-based techniques quantify the various aspects of human capital well, they overlooked some major qualitative facets of human capital. They argued that human capital is a comprehensive concept and not a financial residual. Hence, measuring HC requires a broad-based, comprehensive approach considering it's qualitative and quantitative aspects.

Likewise, Bullen and Eyler (2010) argued that accounting base techniques could not quantify human capital. However, the human indicator-based approach encapsulates both the qualitative and quantitative aspects of human capital and misses some major strands of human capital. For example, Abdullah et al. (2013) considered five major qualitative and quantitative dimensions of human capital but these dimensions are limited. Companies need to measure the facets of employee capabilities that are productive for attaining their business goals. The firm's business needs heavily influence the importance of employees' competencies. This dependence consequently makes it unfeasible to formulate a universal set of measures that will be applicable in all scenarios. It infers that each organization has to strive to identify the most germane measures (Mubarik et al. 2018; Mubarik et al. 2020; Purcell 2003). Likewise, while analyzing the HC-performance relationship, studies consider that all the dimensions of human capital equally affect firm performance, which may not be true in reality. For example, education, training, and experience are considered the main constituents of human capital and affect firm performance equally. It implies that HC measures must comprehensively consider both aspects, qualitative and quantitative. Such measures can help to develop the industry and firm-specific human capital that could be more inimitable, according to RBV. The availability of such approaches can allow the comparison of human capital contribution across firms, industries, or sectors (CIPD 2006; Mubarik 2015; Mubarik et al. 2021).

References

Abdullah, L., Jaafar, S., & Taib, I. (2013). Ranking of human capital indicators using analytic hierarchy process. *Procedia-Social and Behavioral Sciences*, 107(1), 22–28.

Ahmed, S. S., Guozhu, J., Mubarik, S., Khan, M., & Khan, E. (2019). Intellectual capital and business performance: The role of dimensions of absorptive capacity. *Journal of Intellectual Capital*, 21(1), 23–39.

22 Human Capital: Gauging the Ungauged

Barriol, A. (1910). La valeur sociale d'un individu. Revue économique internationale (December). 552–555.

Barro, R. J., Mankiw, N. G., & Sala-i-Martin, X. (1995). Capital mobility in neo-classical models of growth. *American Economic Review*, 85(1), 103–115.

Baron, A. (2011). Measuring human capital. *Strategic HR Review*, 10(2), 30–35.

Becker, B. E., Huselid, M. A., Pickus, P. S., & Spratt, M. F. (1997). HR as a source of shareholder value: Research and recommendations. *Human Resource Management*, 36(1), 39–47.

Bender, C., & Röhling, T. (2001). Ansätze zur bewertung und risikomessung von humankapital. *Modellgestützte Personalentscheidungen*, 5(1), 27–39.

Bloom, D. E., Canning, D., & Sevilla, J. (2004). The effect of health on economic growth: A production function approach. *World Development*, 32(1), 1–13.

Bontis, N., Dragonetti, N. C., Jacobsen, K., & Roos, G. (1999). The knowledge toolbox: A review of the tools available to measure and manage intangible resources. *European Management Journal*, 17(4), 391–402.

Bullen, M. L., & Eyler, K. A. (2010). Human resource accounting and international developments: implications for measurement of human capital. *Journal of International Business and Cultural Studies*, 3, 1–16.

Cascio, W. F. (1998). The future world of work: Implications for human resource costing and accounting. *Journal of Human Resource Costing & Accounting*, 3(2), 9–19.

Calabrese, A. (2012). Service productivity and service quality: A necessary trade-off? *International Journal of Production Economics*, 135(2), 800–812.

Calabrese, A., Costa, R., & Menichini, T. (2013). Using fuzzy AHP to manage intellectual capital assets: An application to the ICT service industry. *Expert Systems with Applications*, 40(9), 3747–3755.

Chartered Institue of Professional Development. (2006). *Human capital evaluation – Evolving the data*. CIPD Human Capital Panel, London.

Dagum, C., & Slottje, D. J. (2000). A new method to estimate the level and distribution of household human capital with application. *Structural Change and Economic Dynamics*, 11(1), 67–94.

Dublin, L., & Lotka, A. (1930). *The Money Value Of A Man*. Ronald, New York.

Edvinsson, L., & Malone, M. S. (1997). *Intellectual Capital: Realizing Your Company's True Value By Finding Its Hidden Brainpower*. HarperBusiness, New York, NY.

Eisner, R. (1988). Extended accounts for national income and product. *Journal of Economic Literature*, 38(2), 1611–1684.

Farr, W. (1853). The income and property tax. *Journal of the Statistical Society of London*, 16(1), 1–44.

Fitz-Enz, J. (2000). *The ROI of hUman Capital: Measuring The Economic Value Of Employee Performance* (2nd edition). American Management Association, New York.

Flamholtz, E. (1973). Human resources accounting: Measuring positional replacement costs. *Human Resource Management*, 12(1), 8–16.

Flamholtz, E. (1999). *Human Resource Accounting: Advances In Concepts, Methods, And Applications*. Kluwer Academic Publishers, Norwell, Massachusetts.

Flamholtz, E. G., Bullen, M. L., & Hua, W. (2003). Measuring the ROI of management development: An application of the stochastic rewards valuation model. *Journal of Human Resource Costing & Accounting*, 7(1), 21–40.

Gates, S. (2004). Measuring more than efficiency: The new role of human capital metrics. Research Report 1356, Conference Board of Canada.

Human Capital: Gauging the Ungauged   23

Gimeno, J., Folta, T. B., Cooper, A. C., & Woo, C. Y. (1997). Survival of the fittest? Entrepreneurial human capital and the persistence of underperforming firms. *Administrative Science Quarterly*, 42(4), 750–783.

Graham, J. W., & Webb, R. H. (1979). Stocks and depreciation of human capital: New evidence from a present-value perspective. *Review of Income and Wealth*, 25(2), 209–224.

Harvey, M., & Lusch, R. (1997). Protecting the core competencies of a company: Intangible asset security. *European Management Journal*, 15(4), 370–380.

Jorgenson, D. W., & Fraumeni, B. M. (1992). Investment in education and US economic growth. *The Scandinavian Journal of Economics*, 94(2), 51–70.

Judson, R. (2002). Measuring human capital like physical capital: What does it tell us? *Bulletin of Economic Research*, 54(3), 209–231.

Kaplan, R. S., & Norton, D. P. (1996). Using the balanced scorecard as a strategic management system. *Harvard Business Review*, 74(1), 75–85.

Kendrick, J. W. (1976). *The fOrmation And Stocks Of Total Capital*. National Bureau of Economic Research, New York.

Le, T., Gibson, J., & Oxley, L. (2005). Measures of human capital: A review of the literature. Accessed from: https://www.econstor.eu/handle/10419/205575 (February 2022).

Lepak, D. P., & Snell, S. A. (1999). The human resource architecture: Toward a theory of human capital allocation and development. *Academy of management review*, 24(1), 31–48.

Likert, R. M. (1961). *New patterns of management*. McGraw-Hill, New York. 242 Likert, R. M. (1967). The human organization: Its management and value. New York: McGrawHill.

Lucas, R. E. (1990). Why doesn't capital flow from rich to poor countries? *The American Economic Review*, 80(2), 92–96.

Mahmood, T., & Mubarik, M. S. (2020). Balancing innovation and exploitation in the fourth industrial revolution: Role of intellectual capital and technology absorptive capacity. *Technological Forecasting and Social Change*, 160, 120248.

Mayo, A. (2001). *Human Value Of The Enterprise*. Nicholas Brealey Publishing London.

Mayo, M. A. (2012). *Human Resources Or Human Capital?: Managing People As Assets*. Gower Publishing, Surrey, UK.

Martin, J. D., & Petty, J. W. (2001). *Value Based Management: The Corporate Response To The Shareholder Revolution*. Havard Business School Press, Watertown, MA.

Mankiw, N. G., Romer, D., & Weil, D. N. (1992). A contribution to the empirics of economic growth. *The Quarterly Journal of Economics*, 107(2), 407–437.

Mirvis, P. H., & Macy, B. A. (1976). Human resource accounting: A measurement perspective. *Academy of Management Review*, 1(2), 74–83.

Mohr, H.-C., & Keilholz, U. (2001). *Human Capital In Der Post Merger Integration*. Eine Studie von William M. Mercer. Frankfurt/Main, Mercer.

Mubarik, M. S. (2015). *Human Capital And Performance Of Small & Medium Manufacturing Enterprises: A Study Of Pakistan* (Doctoral dissertation, University of Malaya). Accessed from: https://core.ac.uk/download/pdf/268878007.pdf (February 2020).

Mubarik, M. S., Govindaraju, C., & Devadason, E. S. (2016). Human capital development for SMEs in Pakistan: Is the "one-size-fits-all" policy adequate?. *International Journal of Social Economics*. 43(8), 804–822.

Mubarik, M. S., Chandran, V. G. R., & Devadason, E. S. (2018). Measuring human capital in small and medium manufacturing enterprises: What matters?. *Social Indicators Research*, 137(2), 605–623.

24 *Human Capital: Gauging the Ungauged*

Mubarik, M. S., Devadason, E. S., & Govindaraju, C. (2020). Human capital and export performance of small and medium enterprises in Pakistan. *International Journal of Social Economics*, 47(5), 643–662.

Mubarik, M. S., & Naghavi, N. (2020). Human capital, green energy, and technological innovations: Firm-level analysis. In *Econometrics of Green Energy Handbook* (pp. 151–164). Springer, Cham.

Mubarik, M. S., Bontis, N., Mubarik, M., & Mahmood, T. (2021). Intellectual capital and supply chain resilience. *Journal of Intellectual Capital*. Ahead of print. 10.1108/JIC-06-2020-0206

Mulligan, C. B., & Sala-i-Martin, X. (1997). A labor income-based measure of the value of human capital: An application to the states of the United States. *Japan and the World Economy*, 9(2), 159–191.

Nicholson, J. S. (1891). The living capital of the United Kingdom. *The Economic Journal*, 1(1), 95–107.

Purcell, J. (2003). *Understanding the People And Performance Link: Unlocking The Black Box*. CIPD Publishing, London.

Psacharopoulos, G. (1994). Returns to investment in education: A global update. *World Development*, 22(9), 1325–1343.

Pyle, W. C. (1966). *Accounting for Investments In Human Capital. Research Proposal, Institute for Social Research*, The University of Michigan.

Qadri, F. S., & Waheed, A. (2011). Human capital and economic growth: Time series evidence from Pakistan. *Pakistan Business Review*, 15(1), 815–833.

Rosen, S. (1987). *Human Capital. The New Palgrave; A Dictionary of Economics. J. Eatwell and e. al.* (pp. 682–690). Macmillan Press, Ltd., London.

Scholz, C., Stein, V., & Muller, S. (2007). Monetary human capital measurement: Empirical evidence from the German DAX 30 companies. Paper presented at the Academy of Management Conference, Philadelphia, PA, USA.

Stewart, T., & Ruckdeschel, C. (1998). Intellectual capital: The new wealth of organizations. *Performance Improvement*, 37(7), 56–59.

Tobin, J. (1969). A general equilibrium approach to monetary theory. *Journal of Money, Credit and Banking*, 1(1), 15–29.

Widener, S. K. (2004). An empirical investigation of the relation between the use of strategic human capital and the design of the management control system. *Accounting, Organizations and Society*, 29(3), 377–399.

Weisbrod, B. A. (1961). The valuation of human capital. *The Journal of Political Economy*, 69(5), 425–436.

Wittstein, T. (1867). *Mathematische Statistik und deren Anwendung auf National-Okonomie und Versicherung-wiessenschaft*. Hahn'scheHofbuchland-lung, Hannover.

Young, D. (1997). Economic value added: A primer for European managers. *European Management Journal*, 15(4), 335–343.

3 Human Capital or Human Capital Readiness: What Matters for Performance?

3.1 Introduction

Although a vast majority of the scholars (e.g., Becker 1964; Bontis 1998; Chahal et al. 2016; Mubarik et al. 2021; Mujahid et al. 2020; Sung & Choi 2014) consider human capital as one of the essential organizational resources for uplifting the firm performance, there is a group of scholars who do not subscribe to this concept. These scholars argue that human capital *per se* is a crude resource that needs to be transformed to make it ready for application into a specific organization. The ambivalent results of few empirical researchers further fuel this opinion. For example, the researchers (e.g, Chahal et al. 2016; Khan et al. 2020; Mubarik et al. 2016; Mubarik et al. 2021; Sung & Choi 2014) find a significant positive impact of human capital on firm performance. This group of scholars considers a firm's human capital as a precursor for its performance. In contrast, researchers (e.g., Costa et al. 2014; Scafarto et al. 2016; Cabrilo & Dahms 2018; Mubarik et al. 2018) do not find any direct impact of human capital on the firm performance. One reason for these contrasting findings could be the absence of HC readiness. Kaplan and Norton (2004) denote that lack of human capital readiness (HCRd) could be a major hurdle to successfully executing business strategies. Likewise, Tjahjadi et al. (2020) argue that the value of a firm's human capital depends upon its level of readiness. They depict a significant role of HCR in uplifting the firm performance in the case of Indonesian MSMEs. The significant impact of the HCR raises a few fundamental questions. First, as to how HCR is different from HC? Second, is HCR part of HC, vice versa, or are these two independent concepts? Third, how does HCR impact a firm's performance? The majority of the research has focused on studying the role of human capital in improving various performance parameters of a firm. However, few studies could be seen studying HCR (Tjahjadi et al., 2020). By addressing these fundamental questions, this chapter fills this gap and lays the foundation to study the role of HCR at the firm level.

The proceeding section briefly explains the strategic readiness, which acts as the basis of HCR. It is followed by a brief discussion on the HCR. The

DOI: 10.4324/9781003195894-3

26 Human Capital or Human Capital Readiness

subsequent section explains the theoretical and empirical link between HCR and performance and offers a testable framework.

3.2 Strategic Readiness

For understanding strategic readiness, we need to first look into the intangible resources of a firm. Kaplan and Norton (2004) identified three types of intangible resources of a firm. First, it was human capital represented as the knowledge, skills, abilities, and talent of the employees of an organization. Second, information capital, comprising of but not limited to, a firm's databases, IT systems, technology, network infrastructure, etc. Third is organizational capital, which exhibits the organizational processes, structures, and leadership.

Due to the implicit nature of such resources, it has always been challenging for the firm to measure its impact in terms of profit and loss (Mubarik 2015; Mubarik et al. 2018). For example, what is an organization's culture or customer service's contribution to their profit? How much can a firm earn by providing training to its employees? These questions cannot be precisely answered as intangible resources may not directly affect the bottom line of any company. Instead, these resources indirectly contribute to the firm's value. For example, a conducive organizational culture may allow employees to focus more on their job, resulting in higher productivity.

In this context, one possible way to value intangible assets could be their alignment with the organizational strategy (Ahmed et al., 2019; Kaplan and Norton 2004). As a matter of fact, strategy plays an instrumental role in creating value out of intangible. Hence, measuring intangible assets means analyzing the extent to which they are aligned with the firm's strategy. As noted by Kaplan and Norton (2004), a firm may not be able to quantify the value of "a motivated and prepared human resource" in isolation as the value of intangible assets could only be derived keeping in view the context of the strategy. What a firm can gauge is the level of training and motivation its workforce has for pursuing a specific objective goal (Chamadia & Mubarik 2021). It implies that the value of intangible assets greatly depends upon its alignment with organizational strategy (Khan et al. 2020; Mahmood & Mubarik 2020; Mujtaba & Mubarik 2021). Strategic readiness, in this context, is called the level of readiness of an intangible asset to support the organizational strategy.

Researchers (e.g, Bontis 1998) name these intangible resources as a firm's intellectual capital. These scholars consider human capital, social capital, and structural capital as the important cords of IC. Structural capital combines information capital and organizational capital together represent an organization's business processes, databases, copyrights, information systems, etc. Whereas, relational capital considers an organization's relationship with its external stakeholders like suppliers, customers, government, etc. It implies that alignment of human capital, social capital, and relational capital with organizational strategy could be termed as intellectual capital readiness (ICR), and human capital readiness could be one part of it.

Given the importance of the concept of strategic readiness, it is usually expected that ICR must have caught the attention of scholars. However, until now, the IC literature neither elaborates what ICR is nor how it could be measured. We argue that understating human capital readiness is onerous without understating the IC readiness. Hence, we put forward the following definition of IC readiness and call for the researchers to explore how it could be measured.

> *Intellectual capital readiness is the alignment of a firm's human capital, relational capital and structural capital with its strategy.*

3.3 Human Capital Readiness: Nuts and Bolts

As explained in the previous section, alignment of a firm's human capital with its strategy is called HCR. It raises an important question how HCR can be gauged? Kaplan and Norton (2004) provide an in-depth answer to this question.

HCR readiness is intact if a firm fully utilizes its human capital to attain strategic objectives. For example, Singapore airplane has a complete full alignment of its human capital with the strategic goals of delivering superior service excellence to the customers. Besides, their cabin staff, even the ground staff is equipped with service excellence skills. If a person is working in the finance department, their way of dealing with internal and external clients demonstrates service excellence. Those who have flown through Singapore International Airline can see that each airline employee is fully infused in customers' service.

After reviewing the literature on the process of HR readiness, we have found the following important process insights essential for HC readiness.

- Knowing strategic objectives: The degree to which the leadership and employees of an organization understand their strategic objectives.
- Organization role mapping: The process of comparing and contrasting the various organizational tasks with the KSA required to perform them.
- Role identification: The process of identifying important organizational tasks, contributing to the strategic objectives of a firm
- Role description: Describing the roles and responsibilities, to be performed by particular employee for meeting the required objectives.
- Role profiling: Describing the nature and types of skills, abilities, knowledge, training, and experience, etc., required to perform particular task.
- Knowing skills inventory: The process of knowing the existing levels of human capital that an organization possess to perform particular tasks.

28 *Human Capital or Human Capital Readiness*

- Knowing human capital inventory: It is the same as knowing skills inventory where the existing levels of human capital are measured, which an organization can deploy to perform particular tasks.
- Understanding the difference between actual and required level of human capital: Such estimation help a firm to detriment the required level of human capital.

The most important question is as to how the aforementioned dimensions could be placed in a systematic process to derive HC readiness framework. For that, we conducted experts focused group as explained in the following section.

3.4 Method: Focused Group

We conducted focused group (FG) discussions to derive the HC readiness framework. We approached ten experts for their participation in FG discussion, eight among them could spare time and participated in the discussion, which is considered a suitable number for FG (Mubarik et al. 2021; Mujtaba and Mubarik 2021). These expert's primary belongs to the manufacturing sector (fertilizer, textile, pharmaceutical, automobile, leather, and chemical) with the exception of two from the service sector (banking and telecommunication). A detailed demographic detail of the experts is exhibited in Table 3.1. Author, along with two research associates, conducted the first session of the FG in October 2021, which was almost two hours long session. This session helped to understand the various constituents of HC readiness process and their antecedents. After the gap of two months, the second session was conducted in November 2021, which was almost a three-and-half-hour long session.

We divided the first session of the FG in two parts. In the first part, the participants were briefed about the HC readiness process and the aims of the study. The were also given the identified components of HC readiness process. In the second part, they were asked to arrange the HC readiness components in a way that HC readiness framework could be derived.

Table 3.1 Experts Demography

Experts	Dpt	Experience	Designation
S	Human Resources	19 years	General Manager
T	Learning and Strategy	14 years	Head
U	Human Resources	22 years	Group HR head
V	Talent Acquisition	09 years	Senior Manager
W	Human Resources Development	10 years	Manager
X	HR operations	14 years	Manager
Y	Human Resources	17 years	Advisor (HR)
Z	Human Resources	07 years	Sr HR Business partner

Experts were also told that they were allowed to add or delete any constituent of HC readiness framework, if seemed appropriate. HC readiness framework developed by each expert in the light of shared components and experts experience were collected and categorized. Two distinct frameworks emerged from this exercise. In the first framework, participants did not differentiate between role profiling and skills inventory whereas in the second group the distinctions were there. The second session started by sharing the previously drawn framework with the experts and were requested to develop one comprehensive framework for HC readiness. After two and half hour's discussion and deliberation, all eight participants agreed on a single framework. Both the FG sessions were recorded and later on transcribed in order to explain the derived framework. FG helped to derive the HC readiness framework consisting of six steps, as explained in the following sections.

3.5 Human Capital Readiness: A Derived Framework

After reviewing the literature on the process of HR readiness by notable researchers Kaplan and Norton (2004), and selecting the most important constituents of HC readiness, we offer a generic HC readiness framework, which any industry could adopt with minor customization.

Below is a step-by-step explanation of the framework.

Step 1: Understanding the strategic objectives
The first step to analyze human capital readiness is determining what the major objective of the organization is? What organization tends to attain with the help of human capital? For example, a low-cost cellular phone manufacturing company faces fierce competition and wants to expand its revenue aggressively by selling the existing products? The firm needs to have the HC to attain aggressive revenue targets. The production department would require highly productive and efficient workers than those who are more creative. The marketing department may require aggressive salespeople rather than long-term repo builders. From this example, we infer that desired human capital may significantly differ by organizational objectives? Hence, the first step for analyzing the human capital readiness is to determine the organizational objectives and strategy.

Step 2: Identifying critical organizational roles
The second step is identifying and prioritizing jobs based upon their contribution to the organization's strategy. Kaplan and Norton (2004) noted that all the roles are essential for an organization, but all the roles may not have an equal impact on organization strategy. Hence, it is argued that firms must work to identify the most critical jobs in terms of their impact upon organizational strategy. We suggest the roles divided into three groups, i.e., *critical roles, essential roles, and desired roles* based upon their

importance. This division will help to identify the roles having the greatest impact on strategy. Further, the critical roles can be sub-divided based on their nature (organization-wide or function-specific roles). Function-specific roles are the technical jobs, requiring specific human capital, which would be limited to a few employees, e.g., demand planning role. Although knowing demand planning could be essential for a few employees from the selected departments, this may not be required by many other employees of the same organization. It implies that function-specific roles require specific human capital, which can differ by employee to employee or department to department. Generally, such skills significantly contribute to the performance of an individual department. For example, the demand planning skills will contribute to the planning department's performance. There are some roles that every organization employee must know how to perform. These roles are directly derived from organizational strategic objectives. For example, in the case of Singapore International Airline (SIA), besides the job-specific roles, every airline employee has a role as an excellent customer service provider and knows how to deliver unbelievable customer service to any customer who approaches him(her). Figure 3.1 provides a snapshot of this process.

Step 3: Role profiling
After identifying the key roles (specific and general) in the third phase, the firm has to identify the types and levels of human capital (knowledge, skills, values, and attributes) required to perform these tasks. This step should address the question of what is required. For example, if the critical role identified in step 2 is "sourcing manager", at this step, anticipated types and level of skills required for performing the task of sourcing manager would be enlisted—*role profiling*. Likewise, if a company's mission is to be sustainable and taken as an essential general role of every organization's

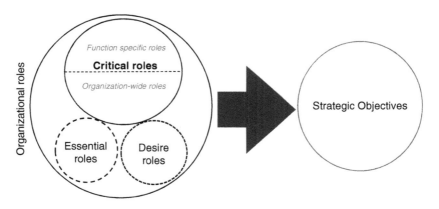

Figure 3.1 Objectives Focused Roles-Division.

employees, sustainability skills would also be critical in addition to the specific technical skills as a souring manager.

Step 4: Human capital inventory
The organization's existing human capital inventory is recorded in the fourth step. After mapping the desired level of human capital with the present level of human capital, a firm can know the deficit HC, which could be developed through in-house development or external hiring strategies (please see Figure 3.2).

Step 5: Gap analysis
By undertaking the previous four steps, an organization reaches the point where it knows the level and type of human capital it requires to attain its

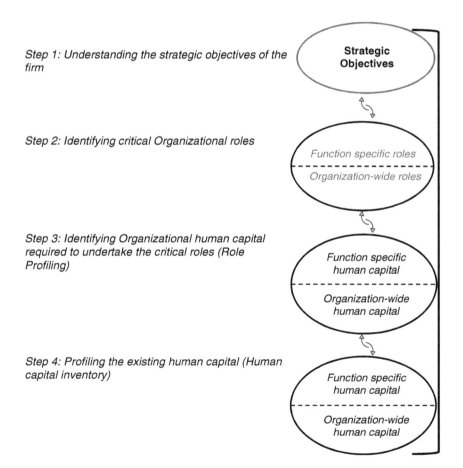

Figure 3.2 Mapping Human Capital.

strategic objectives and its current level of human capital. This allows a firm to conduct a human capital gap analysis by comparing its current level of HC with the required. The comparison unveils the present position of the organization, which could be deficient human capital, surplus human capital, and sufficient human capital.

Deficient human capital means that the firm's human capital level is lower than required. In some cases, the firm may have surplus human capital, a phenomenon where the overqualified person has been deployed to perform a task. Apparently, this looks strange as to why a firm can have surplus human capital; however, this is a very common phenomenon, and several firms go through this. For example, if a firm requires a warehouse officer to oversee the day-to-day warehouse transactions smoothly. A person with extensive inventory management and warehouse planning skills has been deployed to perform that job. This situation has been extensively discussed in HR literature as "over qualified" resource. In very few cases, the firm may have a sufficient level of human capital, well-aligned with its strategic objectives. In such a case, firm has already attained the full level of HC readiness. Nevertheless, in most cases, firms face the situation of deficient human capital. To deal with that, it needs to align its human capital development strategy as discussed next.

Step 6: Devising HC development strategy to attain the desired level of HC
At this stage, a firm knows what it requires, what it has, and what it needs to have more human capital. To attain the desired HC level, a firm must put its human capital development strategy into play. HC development strategy takes its alignment from the firm's strategic objectives and focuses on the way to address the HC deficiencies or surpluses. If the firm has deficient human capital, HCD strategy is brought into action by two popular approaches. First it can uplift the level of internal human capital by conducting appropriate trainings. Second, firm can hire the employees with the required level of human capital.

Figure 3.3 provides a brief snapshot of this whole process of human capital readiness.

3.6 Concluding Remarks

We introduce the human capital readiness framework, which can be adopted as part of the strategic readiness initiative by the organization. The basic aim of the framework is to provide conceptual clarity to the managers and suggest a trajectory for an effective human capital readiness strategy. We have deliberately kept the framework more open and fluid to be more generalizable. We argue that a firm's human capital aligned with its strategy, HCR, is the refined version of its HC and not any different intangible asset. Hence, the firms that aligned their HC with their strategy can better capitalize it and create value. It is also argued that some forms, without

Human Capital or Human Capital Readiness 33

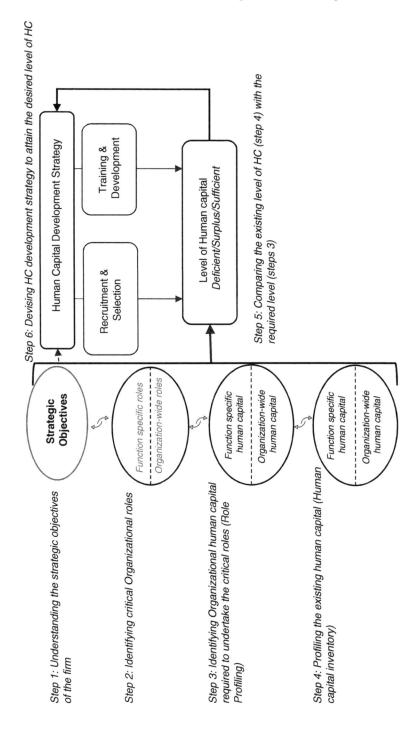

Figure 3.3 Human Capital Readiness Framework.

34 *Human Capital or Human Capital Readiness*

Low Human Capital Alignment with organizational strategy High

Figure 3.4 Human Capital Readiness Spectrum.

aligning it, analyze the linkage of its HC with its strategy create value from it. Hence, there may not be a need for HCR. We argue that the creation of value from HC without considering its alignment with strategy is due to its natural augment with the strategy. There is a possibility that HC of a firm was already aligned with its strategy without.

Before concluding this chapter, we really would like to draw the attention of the scholars and practitioners towards the conceptual clarity between human capital and human capital readiness. While reviewing the literature and having interviews with the experts, it could be strongly felt that these both concepts lack clarity in term of their similarities and differences. Few of the studies differentiated HCR from HC and offered a separate measure of it. Whereas some of the researchers consider it as part of human capital. We put forward that HC readiness is the advance version of human capital. A firm's human capital processed through various steps to align it with its strategy its HC readiness. Hence, HC and HCR are not two different organizational capabilities. Rather, these are two ends of the same scale. Human capital, without having alignment with the organizational strategy, is at the lower end, whereas HC deliberately is processed through various steps to align with organizational strategy is at the higher end. Figure 3.4 illustrates the situations. It shows the degree to which an organizational human capital is aligned with its strategy through deliberate efforts. The left end, light blue colour, shows the low level of alignment depicting a situation where organization has not made any deliberate effort to align its HC with its strategy. The closer a firm moves towards the "high" end, the coloured black on the spectrum, the higher HC readiness it has.

References

Ardakan, M. A., & Ebadi, N. (2021). Measuring the human capital strategic readiness based on organisational capabilities. *International Journal of Learning and Intellectual Capital*, 18(4), 399–420.

Ahmed, S. S., Guozhu, J., Mubarik, S., Khan, M., & Khan, E. (2019). Intellectual capital and business performance: The role of dimensions of absorptive capacity. *Journal of Intellectual Capital*, 21(1), 23–39.

Becker, G. S. (1964). Investment in human beings. *The Journal of Political Economy*, 70, Part 2(5), 9–49.

Bontis, N. (1998). Intellectual capital: An exploratory study that develops measures and models. *Management Decision*, 36(2), 63–76.

Burke, R. J., & Ng, E. (2006). The changing nature of work and organizations: Implications for human resource management. *Human resource management review*, 16(2), 86–94.

Cabrilo, S., & Dahms, S. (2018). How strategic knowledge management drives intellectual capital to superior innovation and market performance. *Journal of knowledge management*, 22(3), 621–648.

Chahal, H., Jyoti, J., & Rani, A. (2016). The effect of perceived high-performance human resource practices on business performance: Role of organizational learning. *Global Business Review*, 17(3_suppl), 107S–132S.

Chamadia, S., & Mubarik, M. S. (2021). Assessing the effectiveness of vocational training programs in Pakistan: An experimental study. *Education+ Training*, 63(5), 665–678.

Costa, R. V., Fernández-Jardon Fernández, C., & Figueroa Dorrego, P. (2014). Critical elements for product innovation at Portuguese innovative SMEs: An intellectual capital perspective. *Knowledge Management Research & Practice*, 12(3), 322–338.

Kaplan, R.S. and Norton, D.P. (2004). *Strategy Maps: Converting Intangible Assets into Tangible Outcomes*. Hadvard Business Press, Boston, Massachusetts.

Khan, M. M., Mubarik, M. S., & Islam, T. (2020). Leading the innovation: Role of trust and job crafting as sequential mediators relating servant leadership and innovative work behavior. *European Journal of Innovation Management*. head-of-print. head-of-print. 10.1108/EJIM-05-2020-0187

Mahmood, T., & Mubarik, M. S. (2020). Balancing innovation and exploitation in the fourth industrial revolution: Role of intellectual capital and technology absorptive capacity. *Technological Forecasting and Social Change*, 160, 120248.

Mubarik, M. S. (2015). *Human capital and performance of small & medium manufacturing enterprises: A study of Pakistan* (Doctoral dissertation, University of Malaya). Accessed from: https://core.ac.uk/download/pdf/268878007.pdf (February 2020).

Mubarik, S., Chandran, V. G. R., & Devadason, E. S. (2016). Relational capital quality and client loyalty: Firm-level evidence from pharmaceuticals, Pakistan. *The learning organization*, 23(1), 43–60.

Mubarik, M. S., Govindaraju, C., & Devadason, E. S. (2016). Human capital development for SMEs in Pakistan: Is the "one-size-fits-all" policy adequate?. *International Journal of Social Economics*, 43(8), 804–822.

Mubarik, M. S., Chandran, V. G. R., & Devadason, E. S. (2018). Measuring human capital in small and medium manufacturing enterprises: What matters?. *Social Indicators Research*, 137(2), 605–623.

Mubarik, M. S., Devadason, E. S., & Govindaraju, C. (2020). Human capital and export performance of small and medium enterprises in Pakistan. *International Journal of Social Economics*, 47(5), 643–662.

Mubarik, M. S., & Naghavi, N. (2020). Human capital, green energy, and technological innovations: Firm-level analysis. In *Econometrics of Green Energy Handbook* (pp. 151–164). Springer, Cham.

Mubarik, M. S., Bontis, N., Mubarik, M., & Mahmood, T. (2021). Intellectual capital and supply chain resilience. *Journal of Intellectual Capital*. Ahead of print. 10.1108/JIC-06-2020-0206

Mubarik, M. S., Kazmi, S. H. A., & Zaman, S. I. (2021). Application of gray DEMATEL-ANP in green-strategic sourcing. *Technology in Society*, 64, 101524.

Mujtaba, M., & Mubarik, M. S. (2021). Talent management and organizational sustainability: Role of sustainable behaviour. *International Journal of Organizational Analysis*, 30(2), 389–407.

Mujahid, S., Mubarik, S., & Naghavi, N. (2019). Prioritizing dimensions of entrepreneurial ecosystem: A proposed framework. *Journal of Global Entrepreneurship Research*, 9(1), 1–21.

Mujahid, S., Mubarik, M. S., & Naghavi, N. (2020). Developing entrepreneurial intentions: What matters? *Middle East Journal of Management*, 7(1), 41–59. *(ESCI & Scopus Indexed)*.

Scafarto, V., Ricci, F., & Scafarto, F. (2016). Intellectual capital and firm performance in the global agribusiness industry: The moderating role of human capital. *Journal of Intellectual Capital*, 17(3), 530–552.

Sung, S. Y., & Choi, J. N. (2014). Multiple dimensions of human resource development and organizational performance. *Journal of Organizational Behavior*, 35(6), 851–870.

Tjahjadi, B., Soewarno, N., Nadyaningrum, V., & Aminy, A. (2020). Human capital readiness and global market orientation in Indonesian Micro-, Small-and-Medium-sized Enterprises business performance. *International Journal of Productivity and Performance Management*, 71(1), 79–99.

Vrchota, J., Mařiková, M., Řehoř, P., Rolínek, L., & Toušek, R. (2019). Human resources readiness for industry 4.0. *Journal of Open Innovation: Technology, Market, and Complexity*, 6(1), 3.

4 Human Capital and Internationalization

4.1 Introduction

Internationalization is linked with the cross-border business activities of a firm. Benito's et al. (2009, p. 1458) define internalization as *"the organizational arrangements that a company uses to conduct international business activities relating to the activities performed in particular locations at a given time"*. Entering into a foreign market provides unique opportunities to the firms by expanding their markets. Several firms, be it small or large, adopt internationalization as a key international growth strategy.

Despite numerous anecdotes and studies applauding the role of human capital in performance, it is harder to conclude how human capital impacts a firm's international performance. Sarala et al. (2019), in this regard, note, *"the role of human capital in cross-border M&A [mergers and acquistions] is an underdeveloped area and requiring extensive exploration"*. This chapter attempts to fill this gap by explaining the linkage of various cords of human capital with different international entry modes.

Drawing upon Mubarik et al. (2016), we argue that varying nature and type of human capital would be required for various modes of international entry. For example, if a firm intends to enter in a partnership/alliance with any foreign firm to capitalize on a global market, the relationship skills of human capital would play a pivotal role. Likewise, for cross-border acquisitions, a firm may overwhelmingly rely upon the exaptive capabilities—*the capabilities acquired during domestic operations that can be redeployed in cross-border activities*. The changing needs of human capabilities thus require the firm to identify the right combination of human capital and adopt a strategy to develop it (Ahmed et al. 2021; Mujtaba & Mubarik 2021). This is in sharp contrast with the one-fits-all strategy, where human resources are harnessed irrespective of knowing what is required to be developed. We supported our argument with the help of data collected from 20 internationalization experts and analyzed using analytical hierarchal process (AHP).

Before discussing how human capital can influence a firm's internalization performance, it is pertinent to explain the various types of internationalization. This explanation helps us examine the linkage of human capital with the

DOI: 10.4324/9781003195894-4

38   *Human Capital and Internationalization*

individual types of internationalization in section 4.3 of the chapter. Based on the previous discussion, the findings on the survey have been presented in section 4.4 and further discussed and concluded in the last section, i.e., 4.5.

4.2 Types of Internationalization

For Yang et al. (2020, p. 1-2), *"[a firm may] choose to serve the market of the host country, through various channels such as exporting, relocation, setting up a factory through foreign direct investment (FDI), merging with or acquiring (M&A) a local company, forming a joint venture with local firms, or licensing of superior, more cost-effective technologies to local firms"*. Primaryly, there are two major routes to enter the foreign market: equity and non-equity modes. In the former mode of entry, a firm undertakes direct ownership, partially or fully, in the host country by building some production facilities, etc. Direct investment and joint ventures are two prominent equity-based entry modes. In the non-equity mode, firms do not directly own any asset in the host country. Exporting, licensing, franchising, and partnerships are the major non-equity-based entry modes. Although literature posits various types of internationalization, also called the international market entry modes (IMEM), five are considered prominent.

4.2.1 Export

Marketing and selling domestically produced goods to other countries without directly operating in particular countries is called export. It is considered an easy way of entering into the international market as it does not demand extensive investment in the host country in the form of developing production facilities etc. The major cost associated with exporting is marketing cost—the cost associated with marketing and selling a product in the international market. Exporting is considered the first step towards the international market, and the majority of the firms start their internationalization journey using this mode of entry. Companies tend to develop contractual arrangements in the host country for marketing and distributing their products (Reza et al. 2020).

Nevertheless, the exporting firms face some major challenges in the form of limited control over their product distribution in the international market coupled with high transportation-related costs (Mubarik et al. 2020). Given the post-pandemic scenario, where severe supply chain disruption and panic buying has resulted in a chaotic situation, and the shipping cost has increased manifold, it becomes more challenging for the exporters to deliver the product at the right price and time (Kusi-Sarpong et al. 2022). In addition, many countries have imposed various types of tariffs on imports, which an exporter has to pay to reach that market. Likewise, export may not offer a first-hand experience and an in-depth understanding of the export market in terms of fast-moving trends, customs, norms, and values, debarring a firm to develop the customized products according to the preferences of the host country. These all challenges require a firm to not only be more proactive in terms of its planning but also adopt innovative approaches to keep the international markets intact.

4.2.2 Licensing and Franchising

Another non-equity-based mode of entry is franchising, where a franchiser sells rights of its brand to a franchisee for setting up a new franchise using the brand name. The newly established franchise must be identical to the original business, following the terms and conditions set by the franchiser. According to the International Franchise Association [IFA] (2021), *"A franchise (or franchising) is a method of distributing products or services involving a franchisor, who establishes the brand's trademark or trade name and a business system, and a franchisee, who pays a royalty and often an initial fee for the right to do business under the franchisor's name and system"*. There are two types of franchising, i.e., business format franchising and product distribution franchising. In the case of the former, the franchiser provides a complete business structure or operating system to the franchisee organization. It may also include the expertise for site selection, training and development of the staff, standard operating procedures, quality control standards, and other allied business advisories. Whereas in the product/service distribution franchising, the previously discussed supports are either not offered by the franchiser or at a very limited level (IFA 2021). Fast food restaurants like Burger King and Subway, and retail stores like 7-Eleven are some examples of business format franchising.

In contrast to franchising, licensing has a limited involvement of the Licensor in the licensee business. Licensing authorizes a specific company to utilize the intellectual property (technological know-how, trademark, design, and patents) of a licensor against agreed royalty. One major example of licensing is the famous brand Calvin Klein, working with various manufacturers by giving them licenses to use its brand for selling the product.

Licensing, especially technological licensing, appears as a major internationalization strategy. A plethora of literature documents the financial gains accrued through technological licensing. For example, the study of Vishwasrao (2007) exhibits that firms in the United States received around 12 billion dollars by licensing their technologies to foreign firms in 2002. Now, after almost 20 years, the amount could be in hundreds of billions of dollars. This evidence shows that licensing constitutes one of the major chunks in the non-equity-based entry mode transactions.

4.2.3 Cross-border Mergers and Acquisitions

The acquisition is described as acquiring control of a foreign firm by purchasing its ownership through buying stocks or direct payment to the owners if it's a private firm. It is interesting to note that cross-border acquisitions constitute 60% of the total global acquisitions, hence, appearing as a significant and strategic move to expand internationally. However, it is debatable what kind of objectives the firm associates with its cross-border acquisition. Researchers unanimously agree about the strategic significance of the *acquisitions* in a firm's international growth voyage. The company prefers an acquisition strategy due to its ability to quickly access an established market. It is also a preferred strategy when the firm wants to attain economies of scale. Nonetheless, the acquisition is also considered an expensive and risky international entry mode especially in the countries with the stronger local currency. Further, acquiring foreign firms also demands a thorough understanding of the host country's laws, rules, and regulations (Mubarik et al. 2021). In addition to it, the local legitimacy, by following the local customs practices, also plays a critical role in the success and failure of acquisitions.

In contrast, a merger is when two companies merge into one to form a legal entity. According to (2018, United Nations Conference on Trade and Development [UNCTAD](2010) merger control guidelines, *"[a merger] is generally defined as a fusion between two or more enterprises previously independent of each other, whereby the identity of one or more is lost, and the result is a single enterprise"*. The merging firms usually bear almost, not exactly, identical size, and customers base.

One of the renowned mergers was between Daimler-Benz and Chrysler, where both companies were merged to form a new company called DaimlerChrysler in 1998. Both firms surrendered their stocks to issue new stock (Daimler 2021). Daimler considers it one of the key strategic moves, mentioning, "The merger with the Chrysler Corporation and the taking of stakes in the Asian automakers Mitsubishi Motors and Hyundai Motor Company had pursued the aim of making the company a world-leading automotive group" (Daimler 2021). Following are some major kinds of mergers:

- **Conglomerate merger**: When two companies from different backgrounds merge to form a new company.
- **Congeneric**: It represents a kind of merger where two companies with different products and/or services serve the same market. Broadcom and Mobilink merger is one of the examples of the congeneric merger.
- **Concentric merger**: The merger of two firms operating in the same industry to provide an extended product for serving the broader demands of customers.
- **Horizontal merger**: Where two firms, sharing the same products and markers and having direct competition with each merge together to form a new entity.
- **Vertical merger**: A merger with the suppliers or customer company. This is used as a backward and/or forward integrations strategy.

4.2.4 Joint Ventures and Wholly Owned Subsidiary

Before explaining joint ventures and wholly owned subsidiaries, it is essential to shedding light on greenfield investment. It entails international entry through which a firm directly develops its business operations, distribution networks, and other facilities in the foreign market. This could be done directly by forming a wholly owned subsidiary or through joint venture projects. Greenfield investment differs from mergers and acquisitions as it involves the direct undertaking of the business operational activities by developing from the foundations. Although greenfield investments are risky and costly propositions, they offer reasonable control.

Greenfield investment could be made through joint ventures (JV) or by owning a subsidiary in the foreign country, *interalia*. A joint venture is an agreement of two firms to jointly undertake a project for profit. In order to reduce the risk of newness in the market and capitalize on the strength of each other, several firms join hands together with the local firms to form a joint venture project for targeting a foreign market. For a successful joint venture, a firm must share risk, resources, and dealings with rules and regulations. In some countries, governments out restriction to hold wholly owned subsidiaries; hence, JV appears the most suitable strategy to deal with such local restrictions.

According to Dailami et al. (2012, p. 6), *"When companies venture abroad, they often first establish a small foothold in new markets through branch or representative offices, small distribution networks, or maintenance centers. Such small greenfield investments can be the first step toward execution of a firm's globalization strategy, allowing companies with limited international exposure to gain experience and local knowledge before making a major commitment to a particular market through an outright acquisition or large-scale investment via mergers".*

The wholly owned subsidiary (WoS), as it reflects from its name, is the type of entry mode where a firm holds full ownership of its foreign entity. A firm can have two primary options to own a WoS: acquisition or greenfield investment projects. Depending on market conditions and business dynamics, a firm chooses the entry mode to own WoS in a foreign market. Owning a full subsidiary in a foreign country is considered a suitable strategy for changing market dynamics. Volkswagen AG is one of the prominent companies having wholly owned subsidiaries in many countries.

In short, joint ventures and WOS could be two major international equity-based entry modes.

4.3 Human Capital and Internationalization

In the earlier part of the book, we briefly discussed human capital as the knowledge skills and abilities of an organization's employees, which can be operationalized by the nine major dimensions and 36 sub-dimensions exhibited in Mubarik et al. (2018). Drawing upon the resource-based theory and human capital theory, we argue that a firm's human capital can help it have superior international performance. It has been well-established in the literature, as noted by Mubarik et al. (2020). Nevertheless, we argue that specific human capital required for an international venture differs by its entry mode. Our first argument is that the specific type of human capital needed for equity-based entry may differ from non-equity-based entry. Starting from the exports, a major non-equity-based entry mode, we put forward that human capital skills like international marketing, customers' relationship management, communication, and knowledge about the international markets demand pattern, rules, regulations, and changing dynamics may significantly help an organization to tap the international export market. The priority of these skills remains higher for uplifting the firm's exports as compared to other entry barriers.

On the contrary, if a firm plans to acquire a foreign subsidiary, the type, and intensity of the human capital may significantly be different than exports. Since acquisition involves taking control of foreign operations located in a geographically dispersed country, a firm's exaptive human capital may bear more importance than the conventional skills. Here, it does not imply that the aforementioned skills become irrelevant in acquisitions—instead, the relative significance of exaptive skills increases. The fundamental reason may be the significant difference between firms and the host country's domestic culture, institutions, geography, and norms (Cheng et al. 2020). In addition to the cultural difference at the country level, a firm also has to face the corporate cultural difference, named as "double-layered acculturation" by Santangelo and Stucchi (2018). It implies that a firm's human capital capabilities related to understanding the foreign country's culture can play a significant role in both cross-border mergers and acquisitions.

The capabilities of communication and coordination could be crucial for cross-border activities. We name the re-utilization of the HC capabilities, attained domestically, in internationalization as expative human capital. The concept is not new and has already been used by Santangelo and Stucchi (2018) in their seminal work on the application exaptation in international business. They argued that firms develop their human capital for better communication, control, and coordination capabilities to reduce transaction costs of coordination in domestically dispersed units. Applying these domestically acquired capabilities in cross-border activities can reap significant benefits to the organizations as noted by Santangelo and Stucchi (2018) and Mubarik et al. (2021).

The significant role of exaptive capabilities in cross-border activities compared to the important role of international marketing skills in the export reveals that there may be a differing requirement of human capital for different types of international activities. Thus, instead of an organization's one-fits-all policy, it may need to develop specific types and levels of human capital for improving global performance. Figures 4.1 and 4.2 display our conceptual argument (Figure 4.3).

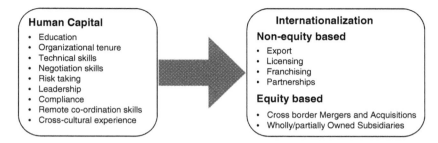

Figure 4.1 Human Capital and Internalization Framework.

4.4 Findings and Discussions

To examine our proposition, we took the opinion of international business experts through a bi-polar questionnaire. The details of the experts appear in Table 4.1. The expert opinions were then processed through the analytical hierarchal process (AHP), and the following results were obtained. The details have been placed in Exhibit 4.1, whereas the analysis findings appear in Table 4.2.

The findings of the AHP survey based upon the opinion of 34 experts globally has been exhibited in Table 4.2. The findings reveal the differing relative importance of various HC dimensions in context of their requirement for entry-based equity modes and non-equity-based entry modes.

Our results reveal that for EBEM, a firm requires a broader set of human capital, each bearing relatively equal importance than the NEBEM. For example, in the relative priorities, organizational tenure has almost two-fold importance (0.25) in the NEBEM compared to EBEM (0.12). It does not show that organizational tenure is lesser important in EBEM. Instead, it shows that organizational tenure may not compensate for the absence of other HC dimensions.

Further, in some cases, higher expertise in some cords of human capital may be required.

4.5 Conclusion and Implications

The study brings forth and confirms the argument that human capital architecture, depth breadth, and relative importance of its various cords can differ by the entry mode that a firm adopts. With the help of an expert surgery, taking into account the opinion of season's internationalization experts across Asia, we conclude that human capital dimensions for EBEM differ from NEBEM whereas a higher level of diversity is required in EBEM. Our findings also confirm the importance of various types of

44 *Human Capital and Internationalization*

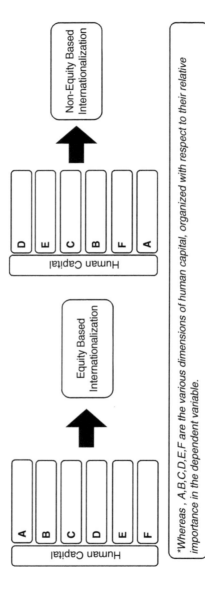

Figure 4.2 Human Capital Requirement Model.

Human Capital and Internationalization 45

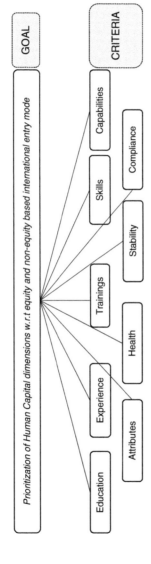

Figure 4.3 AHP Hierarchy of Human Capital Dimensions.

46 Human Capital and Internationalization

Table 4.1 Experts Demography

Experts	Designation	Experience	Country
Industry Professional			
A	CEO	29 years	Pakistan
B	Director	25 years	India
C	Deputy Director	26 years	India
D	General Manager	23 years	Malaysia
E	Deputy General Manager	19 years	China
F	Adviser	35 years	Pakistan
G	Vice President	22 years	China
Academician			
A	Professor of International Business	18 years	India
B	Professor of Strategic Management	21 years	Pakistan
C	Professor of International Business	26 years	Malaysia
D	Professor of International Strategies	13 years	China
E	Senior Research Fellow	28 years	Japan
F	Associate Professor	16 years	South Korea
G	Associate Professor	19 years	Singapore

Table 4.2 The Findings of AHP

Dimensions	Relative Priorities		Difference
Education	0.11	0.14	Yes
Organizational Tenure	0.25	0.12	Yes
Technical Skills	0.19	0.15	Yes
Negotiation Skills	0.14	0.15	No
Risk Taking	0.07	0.10	Yes
Leadership	0.04	0.08	Yes
Compliance	0.10	0.08	No
Remote Co-ordination Skills	0.04	0.11	Yes
Cross-cultural Experience	0.06	0.09	Yes

human capital dimensions in international performance, especially cross-border mergers and acquisitions (M&As).

As noted by Kiessling et al. (2019, p. 1), "Firms have to struggle with the constant need to reinvent themselves to maintain their competitive spirit and keep up with the rapidly changing industry". The need for the competitive spirit and dynamism is even more important while operating in the international market, irrespective of the firm's entry mode. Human capital development could be one of the most appropriate strategies to develop the dynamism and competitive spirit. Based on the study's discussion and findings, we suggest firms develop an *"entry-mode customized"* human capital development strategy. This strategy does not mean to exclude some human skills or employees. Rather, it aims to emphasize the skills that play an instrumental role in the internalization mode that a firm tends to adopt.

"One research stream suggests that the fundamental cause of cross-border acquisition failure is post-acquisition integration, which is also suggested as one of the key causes for domestic acquisition failure as well", as noted by Kiessling et al. (2019, p. 2). Developing exaptive human capital could be one of the effective strategies to overcome the risks of such failures.

References

Ahmed, M., Mubarik, M. S., & Shahbaz, M. (2021). Factors affecting the outcome of corporate sustainability policy: A review paper. *Environmental Science and Pollution Research*, 28(9), 10335–10356.

Benito, G. R., Petersen, B., & Welch, L. S. (2009). Towards more realistic conceptualisations of foreign operation modes. *Journal of International business studies*, 40(9), 1455–1470.

Cheng, C., Zhong, H., & Cao, L. (2020). Facilitating speed of internationalization: The roles of business intelligence and organizational agility. *Journal of Business Research*, 110, 95–103.

Daimler (2021). Company History. Accessed from: https://www.daimler.com/company/tradition/company-history/1995–2007.html (Accessed on: Aug. 19, 2021).

Dailami, M., Kurlat, S., & Lim, J. J. (2012). Bilateral M&A activity from the Global South. *The North American Journal of Economics and Finance*, 23(3), 345–364.

International Franchise Association [IFA] (2021). What is a franchise? Accessed from: https://www.franchise.org/faqs/basics/what-is-a-franchise

https://bizfluent.com/13356305/how-joint-ventures-limit-the-risk-of-international-business (November 2021).

Kiessling, T., Vlačić, B., & Dabić, M. (2019). Mapping the future of cross-border mergers and acquisitions: a review and research agenda. *IEEE Transactions on Engineering Management*, 68(1), 212–222.

Kusi-Sarpong, S., Mubarik, M. S., Khan, S. A., Brown, S., & Mubarak, M. F. (2022). Intellectual capital, blockchain-driven supply chain and sustainable production: Role of supply chain mapping. *Technological Forecasting and Social Change*, 175, 121331.

Mubarik, M. S., Govindaraju, C., & Devadason, E. S. (2016). Human capital development for SMEs in Pakistan: Is the "one-size-fits-all" policy adequate? *International Journal of Social Economics*, 43(8), 804–822.

Mubarik, M. S., Chandran, V. G. R., & Devadason, E. S. (2018). Measuring human capital in small and medium manufacturing enterprises: what matters? *Social Indicators Research*, 137(2), 605–623.

Mubarik, M. S., Devadason, E. S., & Govindaraju, C. (2020). Human capital and export performance of small and medium enterprises in Pakistan. *International Journal of Social Economics*, 47(5), 643–662.

Mubarik, M. S., Bontis, N., Mubarik, M., & Mahmood, T. (2021). Intellectual capital and supply chain resilience. *Journal of Intellectual Capital*. 10.1108/JIC-06-2020-0206

Mujtaba, M., & Mubarik, M. S. (2021). Talent management and organizational sustainability: Role of sustainable behaviour. *International Journal of Organizational Analysis*, 30(2), 389–407.

Reza, S., Mubarik, M. S., Naghavi, N., & Nawaz, R. R. (2020). Relationship marketing and third-party logistics: Evidence from hotel industry. *Journal of Hospitality and Tourism Insights*, 3(3), 371–393.

48 Human Capital and Internationalization

Santangelo, G. D., & Stucchi, T. (2018). Internationalization through exaptation: The role of domestic geographical dispersion in the internationalization process. *Journal of International Business Studies*, 49(6), 753–760.

Sarala, R. M., Vaara, E., & Junni, P. (2019). Beyond merger syndrome and cultural differences: New avenues for research on the "human side" of global mergers and acquisitions (M&As). *Journal of World Business*, 54(4), 307–321.

United Nations Conference on Trade and Development [UNCTAD] (2010). Model Law on Competition (2010) – Chapter VI. Report Number: TD/RBP/CONF.7/L.6 Accessed from: https://unctad.org/system/files/official-document/tdrbpconf7L6_en.pdf (Accessed date: Dec 2021).

Vishwasrao, S. (2007). Royalties vs. fees: How do firms pay for foreign technology? *International Journal of Industrial Organization*, 25(4), 741–759.

Yang, Y. P., Tsai, Y. Y., & Hsu, S. Y. (2021). Technology licensing, entry mode, and trade liberalization. *Review of Development Economics*, 25(2), 834–853.

Appendix-A: Bi-polar Questionnaire

Dimensions	Scale	Dimensions
	9 8 7 6 5 4 3 2 1 2 3 4 5 6 7 8 9	
Education		Organizational tenure
Education		Technical skills
Education		Negotiation skills
Education		Risk-taking
Education		Leadership
Education		Compliance
Education		Remote co-ordination skills
Education		Cross-cultural experience
Organizational tenure		Technical skills
Organizational tenure		Negotiation skills
Organizational tenure		Risk-taking
Organizational tenure		Leadership
Organizational tenure		Compliance
Organizational tenure		Remote coordination Skills
Organizational tenure		Cross-cultural experience
Technical skills		Negotiation skills
Technical skills		Risk-taking
Technical skills		Leadership
Technical skills		Compliance
Technical skills		Remote co-ordination skills
Technical skills		Cross-Cultural experience
Negotiation skills		Risk-taking
Negotiation skills		Leadership

(Continued)

Dimensions	Scale	Dimensions
Negotiation skills		Compliance
Negotiation skills		Remote coordination skills
Negotiation skills		Cross-Cultural experience
Risk-taking		Leadership
Risk-taking		Compliance
Risk-taking		Remote co-ordination skills
Risk-taking		Cross-Cultural experience
Leadership		Compliance
Leadership		Remote co-ordination skills
Leadership		Cross-cultural experience
Compliance		Remote co-ordination skills
Compliance		Cross-cultural experience
Remote co-ordination skills		Cross-cultural experience

5 Human Capital Development Strategies and Ambidextrous Learning

5.1 Introduction

Although it appears to be a cliché to denote that COVID-19 has staggering impacts on businesses across the globe, its real effects are yet underestimated. Companies are not leaving any stone unturned to cope with the pandemic-led losses and bounce back effectively. In this regard, investments in human capital are increasingly appearing as one of the key strategies to face the tumultuous market competitions and growing business disruption (Kusi-Sarpong et al. 2021; Mubarik et al. 2021). This investment is steered through well thought and carefully devised strategies, often termed human capital development strategies (HCDS). Organizations are putting HCDS forward as the lynchpin organizational move to counter the effects of business disruptions and to capitalize on the latest disruptive technologies. Extant literature denotes a profound role of HCDS in developing an organization's conducive relational climate by influencing an origination's human capital and their collective attitudes (Bowen & Ostroff 2004; Mubarik et al. 2016). The relational climate, which can also be termed as the relational capital of the organization, shapes the behaviours of the employees at the workplace. As noted by Lepak et al. (2006), relational climate can also align the employees' behaviour with organizational goals, thus improving their contribution towards the organization's mission. In short, HCDS, through developing a conducive relational climate, contributes to organizational performance. Despite their significant importance and pivotal role in an organization, there is a lack of consensus on what constitutes HCDS and how it affects organizational performance (Collins & Smith 2006).

Likewise, one of the significant challenges organizations face is maintaining a strategic fit between its exploitation and exploration activities, termed organizational ambidexterity. More recent literature (e.g., Mahmood and Mubarik 2020; Ahmed et al. 2020) denote that an organization must be ambidextrous—*striking a balance between its exploitation and exploration activities*—to compete in the market. Mahmood and Mubarik (2020) claim that an ambidextrous organization has higher chances of countering business disruptions arising due to COVID-19 and

DOI: 10.4324/9781003195894-5

bouncing back effectively. This shows that firms are increasingly looking for strategies to help them be ambidextrous. We argue that HCDS can be instrumental for making an organization more ambidextrous, increasing its ability to maintain a balance between its exploration and exploitation activities—*ambidextrous organization*. HCDS contributes to relational climate as well as ambidextrous learning, wherein both of these facets directly improve an organization's ambidexterity. HCDS develops a relational climate, which provides a tacit platform to employees to have a higher level of candid social interaction. The social interaction due to conducive relational climate plays an instrumental role in ambidextrous learning. After reviewing the six major databases from 1950 to 2021, we infer that the literature on the role of HCDS in improving relational climate and ambidextrous learning is scant. Whereas understanding how HCDS contributes to relational climate and ambidextrous organizational learning is pre-requisites for devising the HCDS-led-performance system. These research gaps act as an impetus for the present chapter. This chapter argues what HCDS is and presents a testable framework modelling the impacts of HCDS on organizational ambidexterity through organizational learning and relational climate.

5.2 Theoretical Underpinnings

We divide the theoretical background of our model with the help of two different sets of theories. First, we draw on three major long-range theories, i.e., Resource-based view, human capital theory, and dynamic capabilities theory, to support the impacts of HCDS on an organization's ambidexterity. Second, we draw the linkage from organizational learning theory and social exchange theory to model the effects of HCDS on relational climate and ambidextrous learning of an organization. RBV (Wernerfelt 1984) argues that intangible resources are a significant source of a firm's competitive advantage. Although the resource base view's basic premise is comprehensive enough to consider the role of all types of intangible resources in attaining competitive advantage, this has been applied to human capital in particular. In short, RBV provides a solid basis for human capital's role in a firm's competitive advantage and performance thereon. Since businesses operate in a highly dynamic environment where the changing market competitions, the influx of various technologies, business disruptions, natural disasters, endemics, and pandemics keep posing challenges and bringing opportunities for the businesses, it becomes indispensable to uplift and develops the human capital to tackle the changing scenarios. Human capital theory (Becker 1964) and dynamic capabilities theory (Teece et al., 1997) offer a strategic solution to such situations. For HC theory, investment in human capital through training and other sources improves the human capital resource and result in superior performance. DCT suggests that changing business dynamics require upgrading HC according to the

52   *Human Capital Development Strategies*

need of the time. It highlights the need for human capital, which contributes to the existing organizational activities (exploitation) and also help to explore new ways of doing business (exploration). Tushman and O'Reilly (1996) stress the importance of maintaining a balance between exploring and exploiting—organizational ambidexterity—considers it key for organizational success. Drawing from HCT and DCT, we argue that HC development can significantly help the organization attain a strategic fit between its exploration and exploitation activities.

Further, we argue that HCDS created a relational climate—a climate where the employees from various departments and levels can interact and share the information—which improves organizational ambidextrous learning and directly contributes to the organizational ambidexterity. In short, the contribution of HCDS to organizational ambidexterity is through two important mediators, i.e., relational climate and organizational learning. We draw the theoretical support of our argument for organizational learning theory and social exchange theory.

5.3 Human Capital Development Strategies

The earlier discussion leads us to model the impact of HCDS on organizational ambidexterity through ambidextrous learning and relational climate. Nevertheless, one crucial factor which also needs to be taken care of is the configuration of HCD strategies (Lepak et al. 2006). One of the key configurations could be high involvement HC strategies, which have been underestimated in the HC literature. Any human capital development initiative cannot be successful without high involvement of the people in the organization.

High involvement HC strategies could be categorized into (i) abilities improving HCS, (ii) knowledge improving HCS, (iii) skills improving HCS, and (iv) behavioural-focus HCS, and opportunity-enhancing domains.

5.3.1 Capabilities-enhancing HCDS

The capabilities improving HCDS aim to uplift an employee's knowledge, skills, and abilities to undertake any task. Two major approaches could develop these capabilities. First and foremost is the training and development HCDS. A holistic and effective training program must focus on the following four aspects:

a   *General human capital*: Knowledge skills and abilities which could be employed across the industry. For example, marketing skills, web development skills, etc.

b   *Specific human capital*: KSA which are specific to a particular organizations and have vital role in executing business operations successfully. For example, a firm has developed a particular procedure for evaluating the vendors. Imparting training to understand that process would come under the ambit of speck human capital.

c   *Explorative human capital*: KSAs that are required to undertake the innovative activities.
d   *Exploitative human capital*: KSAs that are required to undertake the exploitative activities.

To see the extent to which a training program is successful, firm must also take care of the following points:

a   Alignment of training programs with HCDS: The HCDS sets the objectives of all the strategies being executed for HC development. Hence, a training program must be well aligned with HCDS.
b   Comprehensive training: Training programs must be comprehensive enough to inculcate the desired KSA.
c   Cross-functional training: It is important for both generic and specific human capital development.

The second-important capability enhancing HCD strategy could be staffing. It advocates the need to improve the quality of HC through comprehensive staffing processes. It also requires HCDS to grant special importance to finding "the right person for the right job" through effective recruitment and selection. This needs revisiting the recruitment and selection process keeping in view the talent management strategy of the firm, which has been explained in the following section.

5.3.2 Behavioural HCDS

Such HCCDS focuses on the behavioural aspect of employees. The major focuses of such a strategy are the motivation and commitment of employees. These strategies encapsulate all such practices and actions that directly and indirectly contribute to the motivation of employees and help increase their commitment and consistency with the organization. Drawing upon the HR literature, we divide the motivation into intrinsic and extrinsic motivation, where the former is externally pushed and later is internally driven. The major motivation-focused HCDS are compensation and performance appraisal as these two organizational practices directly influence employees' motivation and commitment. Strategically crafted and executed compensation and performance appraisal system significantly improve the employees' motivation and commitment towards their job. Such strategy create awareness among employees that their work is being valued.

We argue that an effective compensation management system where employees are encouraged and appreciated according to their efforts and contribution toward accomplishment of organizational task, could significantly

54 Human Capital Development Strategies

mold the behaviour of the employees favourable. Such system also improves, organizational coherence, communication and synergy. "For Incentive systems based on group and organization results establish a common set of inducements that stimulate employees' motives to build varied relations to obtain information and knowledge, and to apply it to organizational operations" as noted by Prieto and Pilar Pérez Santana (2012).

We are not taking a detailed commentary on the performance appraisal and compensation management systems as both of these concepts have been thoroughly researched.

5.3.3 Talent Management Has Driven HCDS

Talent management is considered synonymous with human capital (Ozel & Karacay 2019). It is regarded as a critical organizational strategy to develop and retain the human capital instrumental in attaining the organizational objectives (Glaister et al. 2018). For Ingham (2006) the prime focus of talent management is to manage the right mic of HCR for an organization through attracting, recruiting, developing, and promoting employees of an organization. In short, TM-driven HCDS is a *"complete cycle process"* consisting of various strategies, enabling a firm to develop and maintain an effective TM architecture (Mujtaba & Mubarik 2022; Sparrow & Makram 2015). The focus of TM-HCDS is attracting and retaining high-quality human capital resources, developing their human capital, and keeping them on the track of continuous improvement.

Drawing from Mujtaba and Mubarik (2022), we have designed a TMS framework that can help the organization improve its human capital. Figure 5.1 depicts the TMS framework, which consists of 05 significant steps. The constituents of the TMS framework may look like the conventional HR processes; however, the uniqueness lies in the way these are being coordinated and executed.

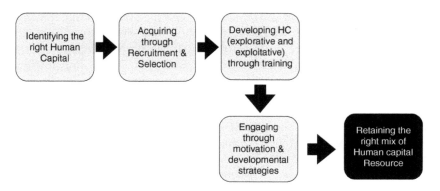

Figure 5.1 TMS Framework.

5.3.3.1 Identifying

The first process is identifying the critical human capital required for performing the significant nature of tasks. This requires identifying the type of human capital required to undertake a specific task. This includes identifying the generalist, specialist, explorative, and exploitative nature of human capital.

5.3.3.2 Acquisition

After identification, acquiring the required human capital resource (HCR) is the second important step in the talent management framework. It is a multi-stage process, which requires a thoughtful and well-planned process to recruit and select the most suitable HCR. As noted by Mujtaba (2022) and Mubarik and Mujtaba (2022), the acquisition is a continuous process comprising four critical stages, as depicted in Figure 5.2. The stages illustrated in Figure 5.2 bank upon the employer outreach, branding, professional networking, and creating a close relationship with the potential talent.

Further, acquisition success heavily relies upon the organization's recruitment and selection processes (Walk et al. 2013). Previously, a university degree was used as a benchmark to assess the quality of HCR. However, the situation is changing drastically, and firms are increasingly looking for skills rather than degrees. Similarly, the conventional staffing approaches are appearing less effective in acquiring the right HC and firms are increasingly moving toward the innovative methods of attracting and acquiring employees. It is also important to clarify that recruitment and selection is a subset of talent acquisition. Recruitment is alone an essential cord of talent acquisition but does not encapsulate all of the essential elements required to satisfy the staffing needs.

5.3.3.3 Developing Talent

The success of talent acquisition greatly depends upon the way it is developed. As noted by Mujtba and Mubarik (2020), it is not sufficient to acquire the talent to fill critical positions. Still, there is a need to craft a comprehensive talent development strategy for managing and upgrading

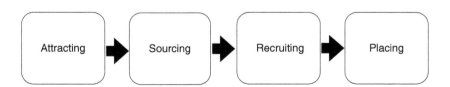

Figure 5.2 Acquisition Process.

56   *Human Capital Development Strategies*

the human capital of this high performer (Wolor et al. 2020). Failing to do so can direly affect that talent's currency and relevancy. Given the present scenario where technological influx from one end and COVID-led disruption from the other end is rapidly changing the business dynamics, it is even more important to develop the talent to meet these changing requirements. These rapidly appearing changes demand an organization's human capital to be explorative and exploitative simultaneously. It implies that the human capital resource (HCR) of an organization must possess the ability to undertake the existing tasks effectively and to be able to explore new ways for doing these tasks productively. Such a type of HCR allows an organization to strike out a balance between its exploratory and exploitative activities. Further, the firm's talent development program creates a win–win situation where employees get opportunities for their career development and firms to benefit from the improved HC of those employees. Training and development are two fundamental ways of talent development. Where training focuses on the inculcation of specific skills, abilities and knowledge. There development is a continuous process linked with continuous learning, knowledge improvement, norms and values of employees. Some practitioners consider development a broader organizational activity compared to training (Ulrich & Allen 2014).

A company can conduct a variety of training programs depending upon the need analysis. This training encompasses on-the-job training, off-the-job training, specific skill enhancement training, and general training. Besides training, organizational climate plays a pivotal role in talent development. For example, learning organizations provide higher opportunities for talent development (Jayaraman et al. 2018; Tang et al. 2018). In addition to the training programs, factors like job enrichment, rotation, engagement, and empowerment are also crucial for talent development. Likewise, assigning challenging tasks to the employees also contributes to their development (Yost & Chang 2009). As noted by Mujtaba(2022), "… *the companies need highly educated and skilled individuals who need to be trained on a continuous basis so that they should be updated and equipped with the advanced technology for innovative product progress*".

In condensed form, talent development through training and development strategies can play an influential role in developing the human capital relevant to the exploratory and exploitative activities of the firm.

5.3.3.4 Engaging Talent

Usually talent engagement is taken in two different perspectives. At one end, it is considered as engaging the potential talent, after attraction, with the organization to successfully take them onboard. At the other end, it is considered the process of engaging in a meaningful job where (s)he can develop an emotional attachment with his/her work. In our framework, we the concept of talent engagement is closer to the later definition. We suggest that the firm develop engagement strategies, creating an emotional link of an employee with his or her job (Amushila & Bussin 2021). A number of scholars (Amushila & Bussin 2021; Gibbons 2006; Yuniati et al. 2021), note that engagement is the emotional association of an employee with his/her organizational tasks, supervisors, and coworkers and it influences an employee to go the extra mile for completion of the assigned tasks. Some of the essential aspects to be looked at for effective talent engagement are as follows:

- Developing an environment of trust and integrity. Every employee of the organization must feel that (s)he is being trusted and his/her self-esteem is considered important.
- The clarity in the roles and tasks: Employee must be communicated about his job role, area of responsibilities, empowerments, and limitations.
- Promoting relational climate: Employees desire to be treated with fairness, integrity, and respect and have good relations with colleagues and supervisors. It could be done by promoting a relational climate in the organization, where Intra and inter hierarchy communication can be very candid.

Besides the aforementioned factors, elements like personal growth and job autonomy are also essential for talent engagement.

5.3.3.5 Retaining the Talent

The locus of the TM strategy is to retain the high performers in organizations. It focuses keep motivating high performers through incentives and practices to extend their organizational tenure. Usually, the high-performing employees remain more concerned about the non-financial incentives; their career development could be one such incentive (Amushila and Bussin 2021).

Low talent could result from two kinds of factors *push and pull factors*. Push factors are the factors within the organization, pushing employees to leave the organization. These factors could be the lack of skills development programs, lack of concern of line managers about the career development of talent, demotivating or negative behaviour of the boss(es), and lack of clarity in the roles. Whereas pull is the external factors, e.g., better offers from competitors, compelling the high performers to leave the organizations for better options. To retain the talent, both elements need to be taken care of. These could be done by offering a conducive environment, job autonomy, career development path, supportive culture, and empowerment. A plethora of literature could be found arguing the significance of work-life balance for retaining talent.

58   *Human Capital Development Strategies*

The following could be some of the key talent retention strategies:

a   Top performance-based promotion;
b   Knowledge-based promotion;
c   Work experience-based promotion
d   Fast track career development
e   Assigning challenging tasks,
f   Job rotation,
g   Salary and rewards,
h   Job security
i   Conducive work environment
j   Respect for Integrity and trust
k   Flexible hours
l   Stock options

One of the ways to track and maintain talent could be the employee's happiness index, through which a firm can gauge the extent to which employees are happy to stay in the firm. An organization can develop a customized retention strategy by considering the earlier-discussed factors.

5.4 Linking HCDS with Relational Climate

A relational climate demonstrates an organizational social environment where employees can freely interact with each other and share knowledge. The relational climate refers to the network of relationships and associations in the organizations. These relationship networks depicts the interdepartmental, inter-organizational hierarchy, and inter-employees relationships. The way employees interact with each other to execute the business tasks. An effective relational climate allows employees to communicate with anybody across the board without any fear or restriction.

Drawing from Collins and Smith (2006), we argue that relational climate represents the level of trust, shared values and cognitions, and cooperation among an organization's employees. An intact and comprehensive set of HCDS strategies can significantly develop the relational climate of a firm, which further can play a significant role in organizational learning. Looking into major HCDS—*ability enhancing, talent management HCDS*—discussed in the previous section, a close association of these three major practices could be found with elements of relational climate like trust, cooperation, and shared values.

Starting from the ability enhancing HCDS, this strategy aims to improve the knowledge, skills and abilities of the workforce through training and staffing. As noted by Prieto and Pilar Pérez Santana (2012, p.193), ability-enhancing HCDS, *" … improves employees' shared cognitive abilities to understand and internalize knowledge by helping them to feel more assured of their abilities—and of others' abilities".* For example, staffing, preferring the individuals having higher tendency to agree on the common organizational norms and values, contributes to the relational climate of the organization. Staffing can also play a key role in relational climate by using "work environment fit" framework while evaluating the potential employee. Further, training emphasizing relationship building, interdepartmental integration, and cooperation also supports the organization's relational climate. Even the technical training provide an opportunity for the employees to interact with each other beyond the professional interaction at the workplace. As noted by Prieto and Pilar Pérez Santana (2012), exhaustive training and socialization can significantly help employees understand their company's shared values, norms, cognition, and philosophy. Likewise, OJTs and cross-departmental training help employees develop relationships and connections with other employees, thus contributing to the relational climates of the organization. General training like interpersonal, teambuilding and service excellence also help employees to develop informal relationships, trust and cooperation with other employees of the organization.

Talent Management HCDS are also a major contributor to the relational climate of an organization. This strategy, through five stages process, refines the staffing process of the organization and help the organization in ensuring the HCR with shared values and visions. TMHCDS, through talent development and engagement processes, offers growth and development opportunities to the employees. Interdependent and innovative workplace design, where interactions and communication remain the key for performing organizational tasks, promotes relational climate and even results in higher organizational learning. For instance, instead of a strictly individualized job, task can be designed in a way where employees can work closely with each other to complete the assigned job. The team-oriented work design not only improves communication and relationship across the organization but also provides opportunities to learn from each other. Taken together, redesigning the tasks for greater talent engagement can positively influence the relational climate and organizational learning. Likewise, participation of employees and empowerment can play a significant role in developing the positive perception of employees about their welfare, trust, and integrity. This positive perception further motivates the employees to reciprocate through higher commitment in their jobs.

Thirds, behavioural HCDS, which aims at improving the motivation level of employees, also play a vital role in the relational climate of an organization. Further, the behavioural HCDS, which includes enhancing motivation strategies such as compensation and performance appraisal, directly contributes to the organization's relational climate by promoting an egalitarian scenario. A well-crafted motivation enhancing strategy creates an organizational relational climate where everyone can communicate without any hesitation. Such communication and coordination improve trust and cooperation among members of an organization, thus enhancing the relational climate. The above discussion leads us to draw the following proposition.

Proposition 1. *HCDS focusing on employees' abilities, talent, and behaviour contributes to the relational climate of an organization.*

5.4.1 HCDS, Ambidextrous Learning, and Organizational Ambidexterity

The scholastic work on the learning organization denotes that ambidextrous learning occurs through an intertwined multi-stage process of knowledge acquiring, sharing, and integrating (see Figure 5.3).

This process integrates the individual knowledge with the organizational knowledge, which further trickles down to the members of the organization (Crossan et al. 1999). HCDS and relational climate help an organization steer the collective efforts to combine the exploitative and exploratory knowledge regularly and integrate it with the organizational knowledge (Birkinshaw & Gibson 2004; Mubarik et al., 2021). HCDS promote the exploratory human capital—*creative behaviour where employees strive to think out of the box for finding solutions to the job-related challenges and novel ways to capitalize on opportunities*—and also harness the exploitative human capital—*the KSA required to improve the productivity of employees*—thus enabling the firm to have ambidextrous learning. Likewise, the relational climate allows inter and intra-departmental exchange of ideas and information. This cross-functional culture greatly helps an organization to be ambidextrous (Mahmood & Mubarik 2020). Putting differently, relational climate sets the backdrop to exchange the knowledge formally and informally. This pretext or setting also plays an instrumental role in accessing, sharing, interpreting, and expanding knowledge across the organization. Likewise, it also fosters cooperation, trust, and shared values, which lead to exchanging information and novel ideas.

Putting together, relational climate help organization to capitalize on the knowledge and integrate it with organizational knowledge (Lubatkin et al. 2006). It provides a platform where employees freely and openly interact

Figure 5.3 Learning Process.

and exchange ideas, knowledge, and learn new ways of doing tasks (Birkinshaw & Gibson 2004). We further argue that organizational learning, attained through relational climate and HCDS can significantly contribute to the organizational ambidexterity. The above discussion leads us to draw the second proposition (see Figure 5.4):

Proposition 2. *The organization's relational climate improves ambidextrous learning of an organization, which further improves organizational ambidexterity.*

5.5 Concluding Remarks and Future Research Agenda

The focus of this chapter was to discuss the prominent HCDS and highlight as to how these strategies can influence ambidextrous learning and organizational ambidexterity. We introduced the notion of relational climate—*it encapsulates the interactions, networks, and socialization of employees of an organization*—and argues that HCDS significantly contributes to it. Further, relational climate plays an instrumental role in uplifting the ambidextrous learning and organizational ambidexterity thereon. After reviewing the literature on the human capital resource, human capital strategies, and high power human resource practices, we put forward three major HCDS, namely capabilities enhancing HCDS, talent management HCDS, and behavioural HCDS, which can play an instrumental role in creating the conducive relational climate and ambidextrous learning in the organization. We explain that capabilities enhancing HCDS help create an environment where employees can communicate and interact with each other. Especially the training and staffing could be two strategic processes, which plays a key role in creating relational climate. Likewise, talent management HCDS helps an organization to refine the staffing process and create the right pool of talent, having an understanding of organization vision, norms and values. Further, the behavioural HCDS, through compensation and performance appraisal systems, positively influence the relational climate of the organization. We further show that relational climate provides a platform for each member of an organization to interact, share knowledge and learn from each other's experiences and expertise.

We suggest future researchers test the proposed model empirically by taking the primary data with the help of questionnaires. The empirical testing of the model will help to derive the relevant policy and managerial implications. Similarly, we also suggest that future researchers deeply explore how ambidextrous learning can help an organization maintain a balance between its exploration and exploitation activities. Further, we could also see a need to investigate how HCDS impacts the broader relational climate, including the external stakeholders and organizational ambidexterity thereon.

62 *Human Capital Development Strategies*

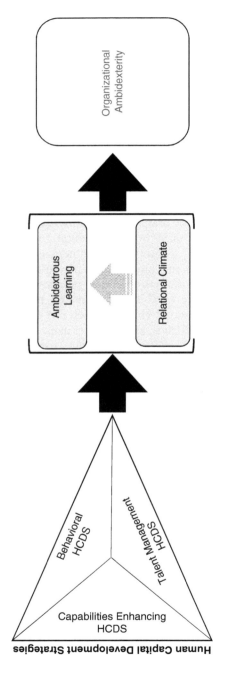

Figure 5.4 HCDS-led-organizational Ambidexterity Model.

Acknowledgement

We are indebted to Higher Education Commission of Pakistan (NRPU 20–11226) for assisting in qualitative survey.

References

Ahmed, S. S., Guozhu, J., Mubarik, S., Khan, M., & Khan, E. (2019). Intellectual capital and business performance: The role of dimensions of absorptive capacity. *Journal of Intellectual Capital*, 21(1), 23–39.

Amushila, J., & Bussin, M. H. (2021). The effect of talent management practices on employee retention at the namibia university of science and technology: Administration middle-level staff. *SA Journal of Human Resource Management*, 19, 11.

Becker, G. S. (1964). Human Capital. A Theoretical and Empirical Analysis, with Special Reference to Education. National Bureau of Economic Research, General Series, nr 80. New York and London. Series, 16(80), 187.

Bowen, D. E., & Ostroff, C. (2004). Understanding HRM–firm performance linkages: The role of the "strength" of the HRM system. *Academy of management review*, 29(2), 203–221.

Birkinshaw, J., & Gibson, C. (2004). Building ambidexterity into an organization. *MIT Sloan management review*, 45(4), 47–55.

Collins, C. J., & Smith, K. G. (2006). Knowledge exchange and combination: The role of human resource practices in the performance of high-technology firms. *Academy of management journal*, 49(3), 544–560.

Crossan, M. M., Lane, H. W., & White, R. E. (1999). An organizational learning framework: From intuition to institution. *Academy of management review*, 24(3), 522–537.

Gibbons, J. (2006). Employee engagement: A review of current research and its implications, The Conference Board, New York.

Glaister, A. J., Karacay, G., Demirbag, M., & Tatoglu, E. (2018). HRM and performance—The role of talent management as a transmission mechanism in an emerging market context. *Human Resource Management Journal*, 28(1), 148–166.

Ingham, J. (2006). Closing the talent management gap: Harnessing your employees' talent to deliver optimum business performance. *Strategic HR Review*.

Jayaraman, S., Talib, P., & Khan, A. F. (2018). Integrated talent management scale: Construction and initial validation. *SAGE Open*, 8(3).

Kaše, R., Paauwe, J., & Zupan, N. (2009). HR practices, interpersonal relations, and intrafirm knowledge transfer in knowledge-intensive firms: A social network perspective. *Human Resource Management: Published in Cooperation with the School of Business Administration, The University of Michigan and in alliance with the Society of Human Resources Management*, 48(4), 615–639.

Kusi-Sarpong, S., Mubarik, M. S., Khan, S. A., Brown, S., & Mubarak, M. F. (2021). Intellectual capital, blockchain-driven supply chain and sustainable production: Role of supply chain mapping. *Technological Forecasting and Social Change*, 121331.

Lepak, D. P., Liao, H., Chung, Y., & Harden, E. E. (2006). A conceptual review of human resource management systems in strategic human resource management research. *Research in personnel and human resources management* (pp. 217–271). Emerald Group Publishing Limited, Bingley.

64 Human Capital Development Strategies

Lubatkin, M. H., Simsek, Z., Ling, Y., & Veiga, J. F. (2006). Ambidexterity and performance in small-to medium-sized firms: The pivotal role of top management team behavioral integration. *Journal of management*, 32(5), 646–672.

Mahmood, T., & Mubarik, M. S. (2020). Balancing innovation and exploitation in the fourth industrial revolution: Role of intellectual capital and technology absorptive capacity. *Technological Forecasting and Social Change*, 160, 120248.

Mubarik, M. S., Bontis, N., Mubarik, M., & Mahmood, T. (2021). Intellectual capital and supply chain resilience. *Journal of Intellectual Capital*. ahead-of-print. 10.1108/JIC-06-2020-0206

Mubarik, S., Chandran, V. G. R., & Devadason, E. S. (2016). Relational capital quality and client loyalty: Firm-level evidence from pharmaceuticals, Pakistan. *The learning organization*, 23(1), 43–60.

Mujtaba, M., & Mubarik, M. S. (2021). Talent management and organizational sustainability: Role of sustainable behaviour. *International Journal of Organizational Analysis*. ahead-of-print. 10.1108/IJOA-06-2020-2253

Ozel, A., & Karacay, G. (2019). Identifying talent attributes for talent management in automotive industry in Turkey. In *Industrial Engineering in the Big Data Era* (pp. 287–295). Springer, Cham.

Prieto, I. M., & Pilar Pérez Santana, M. (2012). Building ambidexterity: The role of human resource practices in the performance of firms from Spain. *Human Resource Management*, 51(2), 189–211.

Sparrow, P. R., & Makram, H. (2015). What is the value of talent management? Building value-driven processes within a talent management architecture. *Human Resource Management Review*, 25(3), 249–263.

Tang, G., Chen, Y., Jiang, Y., Paille, P., & Jia, J. (2018). Green human resource management practices: Scale development and validity. *Asia Pacific Journal of Human Resources*, 56(1), 31–55.

Teece, D. J., Pisano, G., & Shuen, A. (1997). Dynamic capabilities and strategic management. *Strategic Management Journal*, 18(7), 509–533.

Tushman, M. L., & O'Reilly III, C. A. (1996). Ambidextrous organizations: Managing evolutionary and revolutionary change. *California management review*, 38(4), 8–29.

Ulrich, D., & Allen, J. (2014). Talent accelerator: Understanding how talent delivers performance for Asian firms. *South Asian Journal of Human Resources Management*, 1(1), 1–23.

Walk, M., Schinnenburg, H., & Handy, F. (2013). What do talents want? Work expectations in India, China, and Germany. *German Journal of Human Resource Management*, 27(3), 251–278.

Wernerfelt, B. (1984). A resource-based view of the firm. *Strategic management journal*, 5(2), 171–180.

Wolor, C. W., Solikhah, S., Fidhyallah, N. F., & Lestari, D. P. (2020). Effectiveness of e-training, e-leadership, and work life balance on employee performance during COVID-19. *The Journal of Asian Finance, Economics, and Business*, 7(10), 443–450.

Yost, P. R., & Chang, G. (2009). Everyone is equal, but some are more equal than others. *Industrial and Organizational Psychology*, 2(4), 442–445.

Yuniati, E., Soetjipto, B., Wardoyo, T., Sudarmiatin, S., & Nikmah, F. (2021). Talent management and organizational performance: The mediating role of employee engagement. *Management Science Letters*, 11(9), 2341–2346.

6 Fathered Alone Raised Together: A Discourse on the Role of Human Capital and Human Capital Resource Leading to Innovative Work Behaviour of Employees

6.1 Introduction

Innovation is the life blood of an organization. The shortage of innovative ideas compels organizations either to be low level player in the market or leave it altogether (Khan et al. 2021). Numerous instances clearly portray how failure to innovate was in fact the failure of a complete organization. Tesla in automobile industry, Apple in mobile phones, and Google in information processing have replaced the well-entrenched market players. The element that gave Tesla, Apple and Google an edge over their competitors was their ability to innovate. Learning from these instances, organizations have begun to value the pursuit of innovation (Afsar & Umrani 2019). With this active pursuit of innovation, innovation has assumed multiple manifestations. Ideas like frugal innovation whereby firms reset their higher end product for masses (Weyrauch & Herstatt 2017) and open innovation a process through which firms instead of hiding its knowledge share with others to get licensing fee (Chesbrough & Appleyard 2007). One of such manifestations of innovation is its adoption at personal level. Employees' innovative work behaviour is defined as employee initiated introduction and implementation of relatively new idea (Scott & Bruce 1994).

Ideas are basically the results of cognitive processes and these processes are the sole proprietorship of human mind. Of course, human capital both in its individual level and firm level manifestation has to be the most important determinant of innovative performance of a firm (Alpkan et al. 2010). Though both the manifestation of human capital deserved almost equal academic treatment, the current level of knowledge is positively skewed towards firm level human capital. Multiple reasons can be forwarded for this skewness. First, innovation had assumed strategic importance therefore those formulating strategy were the first to show their interest in its pursuit resulting in plethora of studies relating firm level human capital to innovation (Cefis & Marsili 2006, 2019). Second, the construct of innovative performance was designed to measure innovation at organizational level (Hagedoorn & Cloodt 2003). Overtime, there was a realization that taking a collective stock of innovation was hiding more than it was revealing. First, clubbing all employees

DOI: 10.4324/9781003195894-6

66 *Fathered Alone Raised Together*

into firm level human capital may hide the role of individuals in materializing innovation. Dealing all as a bundle has implications both for employees and organization. From underperforming on current job to being less motivated to invest in their development, such clubbing is risky for employees. At organizational level, firms happy with its impressive collective numbers may miss the role played by individuals in their pursuit of innovation. Second, innovative performance of the firm is ultimately related to innovative performance of an individual. Proper harnessing of individual innovative potential is possible when we are aware of employees' individual level human capital both of capabilities and shortcomings. Utilizing the capabilities and making up for the shortcomings of individual level human capital, firms can make a better use of its resource to pursue innovative performance.

The desire to unfurl the role of individual level human capital in affecting employees' innovative work behaviour cannot be realized without considering the organization level human capital. Keeping this snag in mind, the current chapter explores the role of individual level and firm level human capital in affecting innovative work behaviour of employees. But, before beginning and discussion on the role of individual level and organizational level human capital in affecting innovative work behaviour of employees, the two terms need to be differentiated because their apparent similarity may lead to epistemological vagueness and strategical misalignment.

6.2 Human Capital and Human Capital Resource the Siamese Twins

Life either in its simplest form lived by the early Homo sapiens or its most advanced form being whiled away by the current generation is driven by resource possessed by humans themselves. Life in the antiquity was harshly dependent on human's abilities and skills. The gradual transformation of human resource into tools and machinery apparently eclipsed human capabilities, but in reality, human was the main driving force behind all enterprises. With the rise of collective production in form of modern factory setup, the individual human capital was subsumed into a collective unit of human capital. Previously human capital was what was possessed by an individual in form of knowledge, skills, abilities and other characteristics (KSAOs) (Dawson 2012; Mubarik 2015); now, human capital was the aggregation of experience, education and skills of all employees (Ahmed et al., 2019; Coff 1999; Mahmood and Mubarik 2020). This change of signified did not cause much confusion till recent times as our assumption of the additivity of individual human capital leading to organizational level human capital was not challenged by empirical evidence. Two unrelated but important developments necessitated an expedited effort to separate these twins who are apparently same, but their processes are altogether different. First, the emerging field of positive psychology changed the focus of psychology from negative to positive. Now, psychology along with stress and burnout studies positive emotions, happiness, hope and work engagement, in other words optimal functioning of humans (Gable & Haidt 2005). Now, employees were formed and consumed much by their emotions. The additivity of employees was severely challenged either by the synergistic use of resources where total is more than the sum of the parts or ennui causing total to be significantly less than the sum of the parts. Either way, the additivity principle could not hold and there was a need to have two different signifiers for individual level and firm level human capital (Mubarik et al., 2021; Chamadia and Mubarik 2021; Kusi-Sarpong et al., 2022). The second development was the shrinking size of organizations. Knowledge firms in contrast to manufacturing firms are smaller yet more dispersed because of working online. While for Ford motors, employees were almost perfect substitutes for each other, this is not true for a firm operating in knowledge economy. In manufacturing economy, employees were mainly there to provide operating hands. With a little variance in physical power, one person could easily substitute the other. In knowledge economy, the role of employees moved from operating hands to imaginative prowess. Employees differ greatly in terms of their creativity thus the degree of substitutability is heavily curtailed. Following the footsteps of Ployhart and Moliterno (2011), we propose to use two different signifiers for individual level and firm level human capital. For individual level human capital, the term of human capital is being used while for firm level human capital the term human capital resource is being employed (Ployhart & Moliterno 2011).

6.3 Innovative Work Behaviour

The idea of innovation is as old as human's recorded existence in the world. Crises or in benign words needs provide the initial seeds for innovation (Archibugi, Filippetti, & Frenz 2013). What if the idea of innovation itself faces crisis. Currently, innovation has become relative and it has become widespread. First, we would elaborate how the absolute innovation has become relative innovation. In the age of disconnect, each geographical group grappling with their localized problems learnt their localized ways to do handle them. For instance; Eskimos learnt to live in the freezing environment; Japanese beset with resource crunch along with the higher frequencies of natural calamities taught them to live with the bare minimum of resources. In the world of connectivity, the learning has become collective. Instead of fathering invention themselves, nations or people borrow the expertise of others. In Pakistan, when Dengue had first widespread incidence, Pakistani government sought help from Sri Lanka that had already accumulated expertise to deal with Dengue. This connectivity benefits the interacting players not only at macro level, but also at micro level. Ideas like knowledge sharing provides the required connectivity to learn from the expertise of others. The increasing connect allows firms and individuals to get ideas from each other.

68 *Fathered Alone Raised Together*

Along with the rising connect facilitating innovation, the idea of innovation had one more change leading to its widespread adoption. Historically the idea of innovation was just limited to invention that was pursued by the genius while laypeople were there to use the output of this innovation. The relative stability of the 20th century could afford this elitist pursuit of innovation. In the 21st century where change is speedy and all-encompassing requiring a concerted effort by all employees to pursue innovation. Such innovation was necessitated as firms were seeking to improve their processes along with their products. This shift was not out of the blue, the idea of continuous quality improvement was in vogue for the last quarter of the 20th century accruing cost and design advantages to Toyota and other practicing firms. Demanding all to pursue innovation was only possible when the idea of innovation was redefined to make it a commonplace phenomenon. Instead of invention, copyright and patent, innovation had to be the introduction of change no matter big or small. To this end, the idea of innovative work behaviour was introduced. Innovative work behaviour was defined as an introduction and implementation of relatively new idea in work processes, procedures and product (Scott & Bruce 1994). The idea of innovative work behaviour is somehow connected to creativity. It is simpler and broader than creativity. It is simpler than creativity because unlike creativity that counts absolute novelty to be a creative output, innovative work behaviour regards relative novelty to be a creative output. For instance, creativity counts first time introduction of bulb as creativity; innovative work behaviour would regard introduction of the same product in new region or firm to be creativity. In comparison with creativity, innovative work behaviour is broader because creativity just requires introduction of a creative idea while innovative work behaviour demands its implementation as well (de Jong & den Hartog 2010). The second part of innovative work behaviour stemmed from its being common place behaviour. Previously, innovative was pursued by a selected few who had direct link with the decision makers and close room discussion was sufficient for its implementation. Once innovation has become a commonplace work behaviour, the patronage from the top could not be readily provided to so many proliferating ideas. Now, the idea needs championing and support to come to fruition. In short, in its proliferation from top to across the organization, innovative work behaviour has experienced two changes. First, it has become more inclusive by incorporating changes in processes and procedures along with changes in products and services. Second, innovative work behaviour has become a social process requiring support for its implementation (Khan, Mubarik, & Islam 2021).

6.4 Human Capital

Individual level human capital resides in the individual. Human capital is KSAOs possessed by employees to perform their work (R. Coff & Kryscynski 2011). Human capital has two components namely cognitive and non-cognitive; the cognitive component is related to 'can do' spirit while non-cognitive is related to 'will do' spirit (Ployhart & Moliterno 2011). The cognitive KSAOs are broken into four components that are being briefly explained here. The first of KSAOs is general cognitive ability that consists of understanding, manipulating, retaining and creating new insights. It remains stable and determines one's educational and professional outcomes. The second facet of human capital is knowledge. It is the understanding of principles, situations and processes. It can be both generic and specific. It is mostly developed through formal education or training. The third component of human capital is skills that is the ability to learn. They are generic in nature that can be applied to problem solving generally. Experience, the last cognitive component is the ability to apply general knowledge to specific situations. The non-cognitive part of human capital broadly consists of personality and interests and values (Ployhart & Moliterno 2011). Cognitive and non-cognitive facets of human capital collectively explain individual's ability and willingness to perform a certain task.

6.5 Firm-level Human Capital Resource

6.5.1 Task Complexity

Human capital resource refers to KSAOs that a firm can use for unit level performance. The transformation of human capital into human capital resource is not a straight forward formula based process. Depending upon the complexities of process, the transformational process is as simple as summing up the individual units for the simplest work. The process of transformation from human capital to human capital resource becomes complex as the complexity of task environment increases. Therefore, understanding the complexity of task environment is sine qua non for formulating strategies to transform human capital into a useful human capital resource (Table 6.1).

The process of human capital resource takes an additive approach when there is pooled workflow structure. Each worker adds its contribution in an arithmetic sum. In tug of war, an employee added increases the strength of a group by an exact amount equal to his or her contribution. In sequential flow, the unit human capital may add more than its additional contribution or less. If the additional human capital is added to a bottleneck, the benefit would be realized improving the performance of overall flow. Thus this addition can be regarded an addition to each step of the process. If work flow has five steps and the added human resource improves work flow by two minutes, in fact the total time saving is of ten minutes. On the contrary, if the new human capital is added to non-bottleneck work station, the overall benefit would amount to zero as the time saved at non-bottleneck is still wasted by bottleneck work station. Knowledge work follows work process that is intensive. Work flows non-sequentially between team

70 *Fathered Alone Raised Together*

Table 6.1 Dimensions of Complexity of Task Environment

Complexity of Task Environment	Description
Temporal Pacing of Unit Members	**Synchronous Pacing:** All members complete task at one point of time. **Asynchronous Pacing:** Members complete task at different point of time.
Task Environment	**Static Task Environment:** Task are stable and relatively unchanging. **Dynamic Task Environment:** Task are changing.
Strength of Member Linkage	**Weak Linkage:** Little need for communication among coworkers. **Strong Linkage:** High need for exchange of information and experience.
Work Flow Structure	**Pooled Work Flow:** Every individual has synchronous contribution. **Sequential Work Flow:** Work is made up of multiple work units in which the starting of one is dependent on the completion of the preceding task. **Reciprocal Work Flow:** The work flows forward and backward among the coworkers. **Intensive Work Flow:** The work flows forward and backward among coworkers and the people involved have to synchronize and coordinate their related moves.

members and the change from one requires adjustment from all others (see Figure 6.1).

6.5.2 Enabling States

Task complexity presents the demands imposed by environment while enabling states represent the response of the employees of the firm as a unit. Task complexity represents the units of human capital resource. To keep them as a whole, enabling states work like a glue. The strength of the

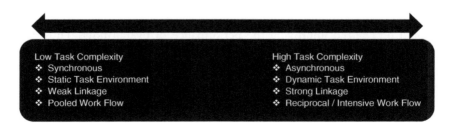

Figure 6.1 Task Complexity—Low vs. High.

Table 6.2 Enabling States for Human Capital Resource

States	Description
Behavioural States	They represent communication, coordination and other regulatory processed in response to the task complexity involved.
Cognitive States	**Unit Climate:** It reflects the coworkers shared perception of unit's leadership, goals and expectations.
	Unit Memory: It reflects procedural and declarative knowledge held by coworkers facilitating their collective working.
	Unit Learning: It is the unit's collective ability to acquire, absorb and transfer knowledge.
Affective States	They represent the emotional bonds binding the unit's members in face of adversity.
	Cohesion: The extent of attachment and commitment between coworkers.
	Trust: The extent to which coworkers are willing to them vulnerable to the decision of others.
	Emotional State: It represents the unit positive or negative emotional orientation.

structure would be determined by the quality of glue provided by enabling states (see Table 6.2).

6.6 Linking Human Capital and Human Capital Resource with Innovative Work Behaviour

6.6.1 Human Capital and Innovative Work Behaviour

In manufacturing economy with a fixed product to produce, employees were trained to follow instructions. Knowledge economy works in an environment that is characteristically dynamic causing a product idea to have a relatively shorter life (Mouritsen, Thorsgaard Larsen, & Bukh 2005). In such a scenario, employees are required to work for both ephemeral fixed product and perennial evolving ideas. Overtime, the pursuit of innovation is becoming a dominant part of work requiring employees to invest their cognitive and social skills in their work. Now, employees are not there to provide helping hands to execute the orders flowing from the top, employees today are thinkers and social change agent (Akkermans & Tims 2017). This change from physical work to cognitive and social work requires human capital to be visualized differently. To do so, we are presenting a model to develop human capital that can be more attuned to the needs of innovative work behaviour.

Knowledge, skills, abilities and other characteristics (KSAOs) are what available to employees to perform their work. Using the terms of Ployhart

72 *Fathered Alone Raised Together*

and Moliterno (2011) these KSAOs are divided into cognitive and non-cognitive ones. In terms of cognitive KSAOs, firms need to train them in generic KSAOs along with specific KSAOs. The earlier focus on specific KSAOs was in response to fixed jobs. Employees knew what they were required to do and were given training in that specific area. The pursuit of innovation requires employees to juggle with ideas from multiple fields. Training in generic KSAOs along with the specific ones would help employees relate ideas coming from different fields. Exclusively training employees in specific KSAOs would restrict the choices considered in pursuit of innovation. Training program poised to build the mix of generic and specific KSAOs would enable employees to combine ideas from different fields. For instance, trained in specific KSAOs, employees would always have a proclivity to benchmark within the same industry, but trained in generalized KSAOs, the number of choices would include those from other industries. Desirous of reducing time required to prepare an airplane for the next flight, the previous within industry benchmarking did not have a significant impact for Southwest Arilines. With the diminutive improvement in performance, Southwest had to search for a speedy changeover example from an outside industry. Their search led them to car pit crew enabling Southwest Airlines to reduce their changeover time significantly.

Along with the cognitive KSAOs, there is non-cognitive component of human capital that consists of personality and values. Personality and values really affect employees' tendency to pursue innovative work behaviour. Despite the stability of personality, organizations can time and again work to create a positive attitude of employees. Two main components of personality affecting innovative work behaviour are openness to change and conscientiousness. They are being discussed separately.

Openness is the tendency of people to positively view change. Individuals high on openness are welcoming to new experiences, they show curiosity and they are imaginative (Silvia, Nusbaum, Berg, Martin, & O'Connor 2009). With these tendencies, individuals high on openness are better placed not only to enhance their cognitive KSAOs, but they can show more creativity. Openness allows employees to try news ways to relate apparently unrelated thus enabling them to be more creative. Openness to new ideas affect innovative work behaviour in two other ways. First, as an initiator of an idea, when others come up with a doubt questioning the plausibility of the forwarded idea, the initiator takes this query as a positive feedback to further enrich the idea. Second, openness to novelty as a coworker helps the person to appreciate the effort and give positive input to further improve it.

If openness is proclivity to accept change, it needs to be bridled. Unbridled openness to change may be harmful because some ideas are toxic. The character's compass that can help people navigate through the unexplored terrain of novelty is conscientiousness. Along with making individuals organized determined, and conforming to social norms, conscientiousness enables

Fathered Alone Raised Together   73

individuals to guard against impulse. People high on conscientiousness are responsible, reliable, self-controlled and achievement oriented (Roberts, Chernyshenko, Stark, & Goldberg 2005). Additionally, driven by sense of purpose, they work hard to achieve their goals (George & Zhou 2001). Employees high on conscientiousness are encouraged and inhibited by conscientiousness at a time (George & Zhou 2001). Their achievement orientation gives them a push to search for venues to learn on one hand. Their conformity to social norms reign them to work on ideas acceptable for society and work setting. At implementation stage, their tendency to follow social norms enable them to wave themselves in social network ensuing in facilitating the required support for idea implementation. So, despite its ability to hinder innovation, combined with openness, conscientiousness provides the effort and direction for diligently pursuing useful ideas.

6.7 Human Capital Resource and Innovative Work Behaviour

Of course, an individual's KSAOs both in its cognitive and non-cognitive forms affect innovative work behaviour. Nonetheless, there is a puzzle needs to be resolved. Suppose, there is a highly valuable human capital, but it is surrounded by a human capital resource that is not conducive for its optimal use, what would happen to such a valuable human capital. To disentangle this puzzle, we need to understand the compatibility of human capital and human capital resource. As human capital resource develops out of human capital, the question of compatibility may seem unreasonable, but it is not so for the following reasons. First, an unused or underutilized human capital may not reach its real potential. This underutilization is aptly but sarcastically described by an Indian politician when asked about the incessant brain drain from India. His reply was, *"Brain drain is better than to have brain in the drain."* Of course, India has progressed tremendously since then and now this remark is not true, but it gives us a message. Human capital is optimally used when it has a conducive environment and then it transforms into organization wide knowledge known as human resource capital. We propose that compatibility between human capital and human capital resource in the context of work is one such conduciveness. Second, innovative work behaviour is a social process along with being a cognitive process. Though the role of human capital resource in augmenting cognitive process would be discussed, human capital resource gelling individuals to facilitate and expedite the social process of winning support for the innovative idea (Khan et al., 2020; Khan et al., 2021; Mujtaba and Mubarik 2022).

In light of the model given by Ployhart and Moliterno (2011), we evaluate the complexity level and emerging process of innovative work behaviour to propose a type of human capital resource that can positively influence individual innovative work behaviour. The process of innovative

74 Fathered Alone Raised Together

work behaviour is not strictly sequential. Employees can juggle between idea creation and idea implementation. These separate processes can proceed in tandem, or in sequence. Implementation can trigger an idea or idea may subsequently require implementation. There is a possibility that while trying to win support of some influential ones, their cross questioning serendipitously lead to another improved idea. Even discussion over an idea may lead to another answer. Such eureka moments lead to new ideas. In short, though innovative work behaviour appears to be sequential, in fact, it is not and both the processes are juggled by employees.

The level of complexity of task environment is determined through task temporal pacing of unit members, dynamism of task environment, strength of member linkage and work flow structure. Each of them is discussed one by one. First, temporal pacing of unit members in innovative work behaviour is discussed. Even initiated by an individual, innovative work behaviour is a collective process (Khan et al., 2020; Mubarik et al., 2016; Mubarik et al., 2018). Multiple employees cogitate over an idea synchronously and asynchronously. Their cogitation is synchronous when multiple employees think over an idea and thoughts and resulting solution are readily shared. In contrast, their cogitation is asynchronous when they think over similar issue separately with different endings. They are required to share their ideas in scheduled meetings. Either way, innovative work behaviour involves multiple people. Knowledge workers have task environment that is characteristically dynamic. At macro level, firms working to maintain their competitive advantage, pursue innovation resulting in an environment that is characteristically a dynamic one. At micro level, employees are not only required to continually update their knowledge, but they are also encouraged to contribute to the overall pursuit of innovation by indulging in innovative work behaviour. Third, knowledge workers mostly work in groups. Time spent together working on an issue results in strong linkage between groups members. Finally, irrespective of industry, pursuit of innovation follows a reciprocal work flow. An innovative idea is shared, coworkers enrich it by discussing its pros and cons, outright opposing it or adding their own input to it. The initiator of the idea goes back and think over the inputs given by coworkers. Next time, the initiator tries to satisfy coworkers while they come with new queries. This to and fro process of idea creation makes it a reciprocal one. The same is true for the implementation phase of innovative work behaviour. Decision makers and coworkers give their input on the feasibility of the idea. Coworkers either support or oppose the idea. Idea is further improved to win the support of the decision makers. In short, the whole process of innovative work behaviour is a reciprocal one as it keeps moving back and forth among multiple players involved. Summing the preceding discussion, innovative work behaviour can be regarded as a work process with high task complexity.

In response to the demands presented by the task complexity associated with innovative work behaviour, the enabling states to support these demands need to be congealing employees to support the pursuit of innovative work behaviour. To start with, there must be a sense of camaraderie among coworkers. The environment in which coworkers work to seek credit for themselves and do point scoring goes against the essence of human capital resource demanded by innovative work behaviour. The role of leadership turns out to be an important determinant of to develop cohesion among employees. Leadership approaches based in morality and with a clear intent to develop employees transform employees into individuals who are morally developed and work for the goals of the organization while seeking to positively benefit coworkers. Leadership genres like servant leadership, ethical leadership and moral leadership are relatively more capable of serving these ends. With trust and cohesion between coworkers and employees and managers, individuals in organization own the goals of the organization and actively adjust themselves to the processes of organization. Of course, they seek to bring changes to the existing processes if they deem them incapable of serving the overall working of the organization. Such an involvement on part of employees and corresponding acceptance on the part of management result in a work unit that own procedural and declarative knowledge of unit's working that in turn facilitates collective working of the unit. Finally, such a gelled unit results in a human resource capital that positive influences innovative work behaviour of employees in multiple ways. First, the resulting human capital resource maintaining trust among employees encourage their knowledge sharing. Knowledge sharing of employees, in turn, increases the chances of emergence of a creative idea as employees have more knowledge to combine to produce new ideas. Additionally, trust and cohesion among employees pave the way for improving the idea along with garnering support for its implementation.

6.8 Concluding Remarks

The overarching objective of this chapter was to explain as to how human capital can contribute to the innovative work behaviour. Likewise, chapter also explores the role of human capital resource the association between HC and IWB. Based on the discussion and theoretical explanation, a conceptual testable conceptual framework has been drawn as exhibited in Figure 6.2. The framework reflects that both human capital and human capital resource affect innovative work behaviour of employees. Human capital allows an individual employees to be innovative and creative in the given asks whereas HCR develops organizational level innovation in the work behaviour. Human capital resource based on mutual trust provides the required cohesion to facilitate individuals' innovative work behaviour. Coalesced though trust, employees find it easy to share their knowledge. This knowledge sharing not only increases number of creative ideas, but it also improves the quality of existing ideas. Additionally, trust also facilitates

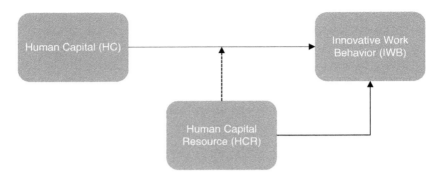

Figure 6.2 Linking HC and HCR with IWB.

employees to garner support for the implementation of the creative idea. The derived framework can be tested to examine its application in various contexts.

References

Afsar, B., & Umrani, W. A. (2019). Transformational leadership and innovative work behavior: The role of motivation to learn, task complexity and innovation climate. *European Journal of Innovation Management*, 23(3), 402–428. 10.1108/EJIM-12-2018-0257

Ahmed, S. S., Guozhu, J., Mubarik, S., Khan, M., & Khan, E. (2019). Intellectual capital and business performance: The role of dimensions of absorptive capacity. *Journal of Intellectual Capital*. 21(1), 23–39.

Akkermans, J., & Tims, M. (2017). Crafting your career: How career competencies relate to career success via job crafting: Crafting Your Career. *Applied Psychology*, 66(1), 168–195. 10.1111/apps.12082

Alpkan, L., Bulut, C., Gunday, G., Ulusoy, G., & Kilic, K. (2010). Organizational support for intrapreneurship and its interaction with human capital to enhance innovative performance. *Management Decision*, 48(5), 732–755. 10.1108/00251741011043902

Archibugi, D., Filippetti, A., & Frenz, M. (2013). Economic crisis and innovation: Is destruction prevailing over accumulation? *Research Policy*, 42(2), 303–314. 10.1016/j.respol.2012.07.002

Cefis, E., & Marsili, O. (2006). Survivor: The role of innovation in firms' survival. *Research Policy*, 35(5), 626–641. 10.1016/j.respol.2006.02.006

Cefis, E., & Marsili, O. (2019). Good times, bad times: Innovation and survival over the business cycle. *Industrial and Corporate Change*, 28(3), 565–587. 10.1093/icc/dty072

Chamadia, S., & Mubarik, M. S. (2021). Assessing the effectiveness of vocational training programs in Pakistan: An experimental study. *Education+Training*. 63(5), 665–678.

Chesbrough, H. W., & Appleyard, M. M. (2007). Open Innovation and Strategy. *California Management Review*, 50(1), 57–76. 10.2307/41166416

Coff, R., & Kryscynski, D. (2011). Invited editorial: Drilling for micro-foundations of human capital–based competitive advantages. *Journal of Management*, 37(5), 1429–1443. 10.1177/0149206310397772

Coff, R. W. (1999). When competitive advantage doesn't lead to performance: The resource-based view and stakeholder bargaining power. *Organization Science*, 10(2), 119–133. 10.1287/orsc.10.2.119

Dawson, A. (2012). Human capital in family businesses: Focusing on the individual level. *Journal of Family Business Strategy*, 3(1), 3–11. 10.1016/j.jfbs.2011.12.001

de Jong, J., & den Hartog, D. (2010). Measuring innovative work behaviour. *Creativity and Innovation Management*, 19(1), 23–36. 10.1111/j.1467-8691.2010.00547.x

Gable, S. L., & Haidt, J. (2005). What (and why) is positive psychology? *Review of General Psychology*, 9(2), 103–110. 10.1037/1089-2680.9.2.103

George, J. M., & Zhou, J. (2001). When openness to experience and conscientiousness are related to creative behavior: An interactional approach. *Journal of Applied Psychology*, 86(3), 513–524. 10.1037/0021-9010.86.3.513

Hagedoorn, J., & Cloodt, M. (2003). Measuring innovative performance: Is there an advantage in using multiple indicators? *Research Policy*, 32(8), 1365–1379. 10.1016/S0048-7333(02)00137-3

Khan, M. M., Mubarik, M. S., & Islam, T. (2021). Leading the innovation: Role of trust and job crafting as sequential mediators relating servant leadership and innovative work behavior. *European Journal of Innovation Management*, 24(5), 1547–1568. 10.1108/EJIM-05-2020-0187

Khan, M. M., Mubarik, M. S., Islam, T., Rehman, A., Ahmed, S. S., Khan, E., & Sohail, F. (2021). How servant leadership triggers innovative work behavior: Exploring the sequential mediating role of psychological empowerment and job crafting. *European Journal of Innovation Management*, ahead-of-print (ahead-of-print). 10.1108/EJIM-09-2020-0367

Khan, M. M., Mubarik, M. S., & Islam, T. (2020). Leading the innovation: Role of trust and job crafting as sequential mediators relating servant leadership and innovative work behavior. *European Journal of Innovation Management*, 24(5), 1547–1568.

Kusi-Sarpong, S., Mubarik, M. S., Khan, S. A., Brown, S., & Mubarak, M. F. (2022). Intellectual capital, blockchain-driven supply chain and sustainable production: Role of supply chain mapping. *Technological Forecasting and Social Change*, 175, 121331.

Mahmood, T., & Mubarik, M. S. (2020). Balancing innovation and exploitation in the fourth industrial revolution: Role of intellectual capital and technology absorptive capacity. *Technological Forecasting and Social Change*, 160, 120248

Mouritsen, J., Thorsgaard Larsen, H., & Bukh, P. N. (2005). Dealing with the knowledge economy: Intellectual capital versus balanced scorecard. *Journal of Intellectual Capital*, 6(1), 8–27. 10.1108/14691930510574636

Mubarik, M. S. (2015). *Human capital and performance of small & medium manufacturing enterprises: a study of Pakistan* (Doctoral dissertation, University of Malaya). Accessed from: https://core.ac.uk/download/pdf/268878007.pdf (February 2020).

Mubarik, M. S., Govindaraju, C., & Devadason, E. S. (2016). Human capital development for SMEs in Pakistan: Is the "one-size-fits-all" policy adequate?. *International Journal of Social Economics*. 43(8), 804–822.

Mubarik, M. S., Chandran, V. G. R., & Devadason, E. S. (2018). Measuring human capital in small and medium manufacturing enterprises: What matters?. *Social Indicators Research*, 137(2), 605–623.

78 Fathered Alone Raised Together

Mubarik, M. S., Devadason, E. S., & Govindaraju, C. (2020). Human capital and export performance of small and medium enterprises in Pakistan. *International Journal of Social Economics*, 47(5), 643–662.

Mubarik, M. S., & Naghavi, N. (2020). Human capital, green energy, and technological innovations: Firm-level analysis. In *Econometrics of Green Energy Handbook* (pp. 151–164). Springer, Cham.

Mubarik, M. S., Bontis, N., Mubarik, M., & Mahmood, T. (2021). Intellectual capital and supply chain resilience. *Journal of Intellectual Capital*. Ahead of print. 10.1108/JIC-06-2020-0206

Mujtaba, M., & Mubarik, M. S. (2022). Talent management and organizational sustainability: role of sustainable behaviour. *International Journal of Organizational Analysis*, 30(2), 389–407. https://doi.org/10.1108/IJOA-06-2020-2253

Ployhart, R. E., & Moliterno, T. P. (2011). Emergence of the human capital resource: A multilevel model. *Academy of Management Review*, 36(1), 127–150. 10.5465/amr.2009.0318

Roberts, B. W., Chernyshenko, O. S., Stark, S., & Goldberg, L. R. (2005). The structure of conscientiousness: An empirical investigation based on seven major personality questionnaires. *Personnel Psychology*, 58(1), 103–139. 10.1111/j.1744-6570.2005.00301.x

Scott, S. G., & Bruce, R. A. (1994). Determinants of innovative behavior: A path model of individual innovation in the workplace. *Academy of Management Journal*, 37(3), 580–607.

Silvia, P. J., Nusbaum, E. C., Berg, C., Martin, C., & O'Connor, A. (2009). Openness to experience, plasticity, and creativity: Exploring lower-order, high-order, and interactive effects. *Journal of Research in Personality*, 43(6), 1087–1090. 10.1016/j.jrp.2009.04.015

Weyrauch, T., & Herstatt, C. (2017). What Is Frugal Innovation? Three Defining Criteria. *Journal of Frugal Innovation*, 2(1), 1. 10.1186/s40669-016-0005-y

7 Beyond Conventional Human Capital: Behavioural Human Capital in Driving Firms' Absorptive Capacity and Innovation

7.1 Introduction

The majority of the literature on human capital theory and innovation have focused on the role of human capital (HC) in the context of knowledge, skill, and abilities (KSAs) dimensions of the human capital. However, in building absorptive capacity as well as innovative capability, firms could be in a better position if behavioural human capital (BHC), characterized by personal attributes and attitudes (Mubarik 2015; Mubarik et al. 2018), is also equally considered. The inclusive human capital development strategy—the strategy to focus and develop both aspects of human capital (conventional and behavioural)—help organization attain superior performance. Human capital to absorb knowledge and information critical in building a firm's capacity and innovation capability requires beyond routine knowledge and skills. Hence the inclusion of behavioural human capital can add significant value to the innovation performance. Employee's attributes, major constituents of BHC, such as creativity, leadership, risk-taking, and intelligence, are indispensable sets of dimensions that have not been explored in the literature of absorptive capacity and innovation. Likewise, attitude, another major constituent of BHC, represented by employees' commitments, engagement, and cooperation, could help build small-medium industries to improve their absorptive capacity and innovative capability. More importantly, public policy's main emphasis being knowledge, skills, and training, the role of BHC has been rarely emphasized. The majority of the past literature focused on human capital essential for product innovation, ignoring the behavioural human capital traits needed for other kinds of innovations, e.g., process innovation (Bonesso et al. 2020). Underscoring the need for behavioural human capital like attitude, Bartoloni and Baussola (2016) argue that technological innovation is a complex process that may require new attitudes, knowledge, and market orientation. Since it is important for a firm to consider each type of innovation—product, process, non-technological—identifying that behavioural human capital is important to enabling employees to undertake different types of innovation. This chapter sets out to briefly delineate the concept of behavioural human capital and its important dimensions and offer a framework explaining how cords of

DOI: 10.4324/9781003195894-7

behavioural human capital, i.e., attitudes and attributes, contribute to a firm's absorptive capacity and innovation performance. We also empirically examine the offered framework by using the data of 614 Small and medium sector firms of Pakistan.

7.2 Definitions and Dimensions

7.2.1 Behavioural Human Capital

We have taken two critical cords of human capital, namely attributes and attitudes, collectively coin them as behavioural human capital (BHC), and examine their influence on a firm's absorptive capacity and innovation (Figure 7.1). There is a lack of consensus on the common definition of attitude; however, most scholars consider it the learned predisposition of a person about other people, objects, or events. This predisposition greatly influences an individual's response to the given situation (Mubarik 2015). It can also be defined as the settled or established way of thinking and responding. As noted by Cascio (2010, p. 46), "Attitudes are an internal state that focus on particular aspects of or objects in the environment". It comprises at least three essential elements. First is cognition, an individual's knowledge and information about the focal object. Second, emotion, feelings of an individual about a particular object. The third is the tendency of action, an individual's readiness to react or respond to a particular situation or object in a predetermined or settled manner. So individual knowledge, emotion, and action tendency are three essential components of attitude. Allameh et al. (2012) argue that employees' attitude is characterized by their emotions, perceptions, feelings, and evaluations about their workplace. Factors like organization culture, values, norms, policies, management style, working environment, and reference groups greatly influence an employee's attitude at the workplace (Armstrong, 2006).

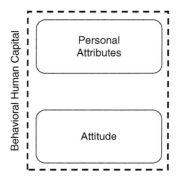

Figure 7.1 Behavioural Human Capital.

The question arises as to what is behavioural human capital and how is it different from the conventional human capital measures? Traditionally, education, work experience, and industry expertise are a few of the established measures of human capital. These accepted measures of human capital do not take into account employees' motivation, behaviour, and embedded skills attained through experience (Bonesso et al. 2020). As noted by Bonesso et al. (2020, p. 2), "human capital also refers to elements of motivation and behaviour that can be specifically related to the innovation activities. In this regard, the literature on innovation management has recently drawn attention to the intangible elements of human capital, namely the soft skills or behavioural competencies for innovation. A behavioural competency has been defined as an underlying characteristic of the person that leads to or causes effective or outstanding performance."

Drawing upon the Mubarik (2015), Mubarik et al. (2018), and Bonesso et al. (2020), we selected employee's satisfaction, commitment, motivation, cooperation and engagement to operationalize employees' attitudes. Further, we argue that employees' motivation, commitment, cooperation, satisfaction, and engagement lead to superior innovation performance. Several studies (Becker et al. 1996; Mowday et al. 2013; Saari & Judge 2004) consider these variables pivotal to a firm's performance. We take the personal attributes as the second cord of behavioural human capital. Mubarik et al. (2018) has developed a scale of personal attributes with five major dimensions: creativity, diversity, leadership, and risk-taking. We adopt the same scale to operationalize the personal attributes. Table 7.1 and Table 7.2 exhibits the definition of each dimension of attitude and personal attributes.

7.2.2 Absorptive Capacity

Zahra and George (2002) re-conceptualized the conventional concept of absorptive capacity and defined it as a process comprising of four distinct yet inter-related phenomena. These are knowledge acquisition, assimilation, transformation, and exploitation, each explained in the below lines:

Acquisition: It represents the effort of a firm to identify and attain the external knowledge that can add value to its processes. The acquisition of knowledge depends upon three major elements: intensity, speed, and direction of firm efforts, according to Zahra and George (2002). The higher level of the firm's efforts can help quickly build a knowledge repository. Likewise, the direction of knowledge accumulation also significantly determines the success of firm's knowledge acquisition efforts. In short, extensive efforts in the right direction can help a firm to acquire the outside

Assimilation: It is referred to as the processes and routines to analyze and comprehend the outside acquired information. The process of assimilation becomes complex and prolonged when the knowledge acquired from external sources embodies differing heuristics than that firm uses. Likewise,

82   *Beyond Conventional Human Capital*

Table 7.1 Dimensions of Attitude

Dimension	Definition	Source(s)
Cooperation	The degree to which employees directly interact with each other and extend their support to overcome organizational issues or capitalize on opportunities. *It does not take into account the collaboration of employees to resist managerial controls.*	Christensen, Marx, & Stevenson (2006); Mubarik (2015); Mubarik et al. (2018)
Motivation	It is the enthusiasm, willingness, and energy of an employee to attain organizational goals.	Rainlall (2004); Robbins & Everitt (1996); Mubarik (2015); Mubarik et al. (2018)
Commitment	It characterizes the extent to which an employee demonstrates a sense of responsibility toward his/her job.	Mowday et al. (2013); Mubarik (2015); Mubarik et al. (2018)
Satisfaction	It reflects the feelings of an employee about organizational fairness, the importance of his job, and career development opportunities available to them.	Van Saane et al. (2003); Mubarik (2015); Mubarik et al. (2018)
Engagement	It depicts the extent of discretionary efforts and dedication that an employee is willing to put in his job. It also considers the extent to which an employee goes beyond his/her core job.	Kular et al. 2008; Mubarik et al. (2018)

if the firm does not have the complementary resources required to comprehend knowledge, assimilation becomes difficult.

Transformation: It illustrates the ability of a firm to transform existing business processes and routines by developing and refining to facilitate the integration of new knowledge with the existing one. Zahra and George (2002) denote transformation as the 'bisociation' process, where two incongruent yet self-consistent sets of information combine to form a new schema. Such capabilities can play a significant role in augmenting innovative and entrepreneurial human capital resource. It allows a firm to recognize the new opportunities and changes how a firm looks its level of competence.

Exploitation: It represents a firm's capability to harvest and induce the acquired and transformed knowledge into organizational; operations. Leveraging from the acquired and transformed knowledge by making it part or organizational processes and uplifting firm's capitates. Exploitation significantly depends upon the flexibility and competitiveness of the organizations' existing business processes and routines. A firm can exploit the knowledge without having any intact systematic processes and routines. However, such exploitation may be short-term. In order to leverage from

Table 7.2 Dimensions of Personal Attributes

Dimension	Definition	Source(s)
Creativity	It represents the capability of an employee to generate any new idea that can add value to his professional task. The creativity also depends upon the feasibility, desirability and originality of the ideas.	Madjar 2005
Intelligence	Ability of an employee to understand, reason and learn a particular knowledge, phenomenon,, situation or process. Employees' ability to learn quickly during trainings.	Mubarik et al. (2018)
Leadership	It is defined as the ability of a person, at any level, to positively influence others in his circle to attain some organizational related.	Chemers, 2000; Mubarik et al. (2018)
Risk taking	Tendency of an employee to take the decisions which have higher potential benefit yet can have fatal consequences for the organization. "It also refers to employees' capability to reframe risk as an opportunity to succeed rather than a way to failure", Mubarik (2015)	Mubarik (2015)

the exploitation for an extended period, a firm must devise the structural processes and mechanisms for exploitation. It is a retrieval process and usage of already created and internalized knowledge. The systematic tram formation efforts may lead to creating new processes (process innovation), products, and knowledge. These form dimensions of absorptive capacity have been further classified into two major constituting dimensions, namely potential absorptive capacity and realized absorptive capacity. Knowledge acquisition and assimilation come under potential absorptive capacity, whereas knowledge transformation and exploitation come under-realized absorptive capacity. A snapshot of absorptive capacity and its types has been exhibited in Figure 7.2.

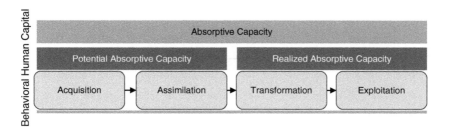

Figure 7.2 Dimensions of Absorptive Capacity.

7.2.3 Innovation

The concept of innovation is often related to Schumpeter (1942), who coined innovation as the process of transforming ideas into commercially viable value. Recent literature on innovation performance measures the degree to which the novel idea is executed and its value generation (Mubarik 2015; Mubarik et al. 2021). In other words, innovation is considered as using any idea, creativity, or novelty to develop or/and improve a process and/or a product that can add value to a firm (Massa & Testa 2008). Improvement in the firm's organizational setting in terms of management hierarchy, styles, culture or approach like marketing technique, etc. Using novel ideas is also catered under innovation. The majority of the literature depicts two types of innovation, process, and product, and both approaches go hand-in-hand. Figure 7.3 illustrates both types of innovation against the intensity of the innovation.

a   Product innovation is the process of developing and introducing a new or improved (incremental or radical) version of the existing product.
b   Process innovation: It relates to the development, execution, or any change (incremental or radical) of any new business process, e.g., marketing, production, distribution, etc.

Innovation performance is measured using two ways namely output based and output based approaches. Following Mubarik (2015) and Adegoke et al. (2007), we measure innovation from both input and output perspectives in the context of Small and medium enterprises.

7.3 Theoretical Exposition

The study takes its theoretical foundations from the organizational learning theory (OLT), the resource-based view (RBV) of the firm, and human

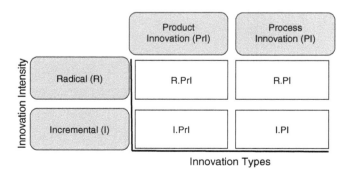

Figure 7.3 Types of Innovation.

capital theory (HCT). The resource-based view (Wernerfelt 1984) considers human capital as an essential intangible resource that significantly improves a firm's innovation performance. Inferring from the OLT and HCT, we hypothesize that attitude, *characterized by motivation, engagement, commitment, co-operation, and satisfaction,* exerts a direct influence on the innovation performance as well as it improves an organization's potential absorptive capacity (*acquisition and assimilation of outside knowledge*) and realized absorptive capacity (*transferring and exploitation of outside knowledge*). Likewise, we also hypothesize that personality traits, *featured by leadership, intelligence, risk-taking ability, diversity, and creativity,* contribute to the organization's innovation and also enhance an organization's absorptive capacity. Moreover, organization learning theory offers the foundations to model the role of absorptive capacity in improving innovation. Organizational learning theory considers learning from the outside environment as a critical organizational capability contributing to the organization's innovation (Dodgson 1993). From the resource-based view, both absorptive capacity and intangible resources (i.e., human capital) are essential contributors to the organization's innovation (Mubarik 2015). According to OL theorists, the firm's performance (e.g., innovation) may differ across the firms due to the differences in their absorptive capacity (Cohen and Levinthal 1990). Whereas, according to Lane, and Lubatkin, (1998), a firm's internal stock of knowledge determines its absorptive capacity. This allows us to model the absorptive capacity (both realized and potential) as the mediating variable in the relationship between attributes, attitudes, and innovation (Figure 7.4).

7.4 Propositions

7.4.1 Behavioural Human Capital and Innovation

Innovation has long been considered as the key factor for the success of any business. Hence, both researchers and practitioners in every era kept exploring the key antecedents of innovation. Among those key factors that can influence a firm's innovation, human capital possesses an apex position. Be it technological innovation in pursuit of product or process improvement or non-technological innovation to improve management, marketing, and other organizational aspects. Human capital has always been considered an essential factor. The majority of the studies focus was the acquired knowledge, skills, and abilities of an individual that can add value to a firm. These researches gave lesser attention to the behavioural aspects

Figure 7.4 Theoretical Framework.

86 *Beyond Conventional Human Capital*

of human capital, especially attitude and personal attributes. We argue that in some forms of innovations and organizational settings, behavioural human capital can play a more significant role than conventional human capital. For example, as noted by Mollick (2012: 1001) and cited by Bonesso et al. (2020), "Especially in industries with high rates of entrepreneurship or where there are few economies of scale, firm composition—the people who actually make up the firm—may account for much of often widely varying differences in performance among firms." McGuirk et al. (2015), supporting the Mollick (2012) findings, note that behavioural human capital may be more important and valuable for innovation in small firms. Previous research put forward that employees' tangible attributes of HC (e.g. education, technical training, and industry experience) and intangible or behavioural attributes (positive attitude, commitment, engagement, intelligence) both play a vital role in uplifting the innovation performance of a firm. We argue that employees' attitudes represented by creativity, diversity, leadership, and risk-taking directly contribute to its innovation (product and process). The higher level of creativity coupled with the risk-taking ability and commitment lead to thinking out of the box and devising novel solutions for the existing issues. Likewise, employee's high level of engagement and commitment help them to be masters in their assigned roles and push them to share novel ways of capitalizing on opportunities or competing in the market (Mubarik et al. 2018).

As noted by Pradana et al. (2020), innovation can be seen as the successful exploitation of new ideas that incorporate novelty and utility. Companies need individuals with expertise and knowledge to develop innovative new ideas. Therefore, to achieve such innovation, firms need competent and innovative employees who are willing to apply new knowledge and experiment."

Against this backdrop, we draw the following testable propositions:

Proposition 1: Behavioural human capital, characterized by attitude and personal attributes, is positively related to the firm's innovation performance.

7.4.2 Behavioural Human Capital, Absorptive Capacity, and Innovation

Absorptive capacity reflects the combination of the firm's internal capabilities with external collaborations to uplift a firm's capacity to absorb outside knowledge. Mahmood and Mubarik (2020) highlight that human capital resources of a firm, especially the employees with high level of human capital in the form of education, attitude, commitment and intelligence, while performing their routine tasks, can increase the stock of the organization's knowledge. Such a type of HCR also develops the relationship with individuals outside the organization having similar behavioural competencies and allows the organization to assess the outside knowledge. Ahmed et al.

(2019) also highlight the role of human capital behavioural competencies in identifying, assimilating, transforming, and using outside knowledge. They claim that tacit aspects of human capital like attitude, engagement, and commitment play a pivotal role in raising a firm's potential and realizing absorptive capacity.

We argue that human capital contributes to the firm's absorptive capacity of the firm whch in turn improves innovation performance. Researches (e.,g Mahmood and Mubarik 2020; Ahmed et al. 2020; Ahmed et al. 2021; Kusi-Sarpong et al. 2022; Pradana et al. 2020) hlight absorptive capacity as one of the major contributor to the innovation performance of a firm. A firm with a higher level of capacity to absorb outside knowledge tends to innovate. AC enables a firm to renew, upgrade, develop and apply the existing capabilities to undertake innovation, whether technological or non-technological innovation.

Based upon the above discussion, we draw the following. The complete framework has been exhibited in Figure 7.5.

Proposition 2: Absorptive capacity mediates the relationship between behavioural human capital and innovation performance of the firm.

7.5 Data Source, Measurements, and Method

7.5.1 Data Sources

The study targeted Pakistan's small and medium manufacturing sector firms (SMEs) for the data analysis. We used the data from 614 manufacturing

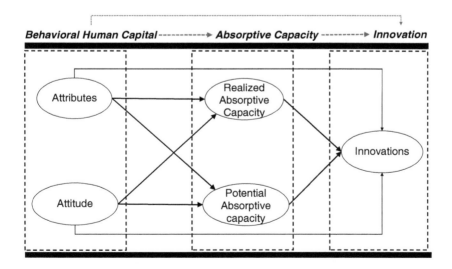

Figure 7.5 Behavioural HC-led Innovation Framework.

88 *Beyond Conventional Human Capital*

Table 7.3 Respondent Firms Demography

	N = 614	%
Industry		
Leather	97	16%
Metal	48	8%
Sports	85	14%
Food	148	24%
Furniture	77	13%
Textile	159	26%
Size		
Small	181	29%
Medium	433	71%
Ownership		
Local	57	9%
Foreign	557	91%
Age		
1–5 years	134	22%
6–10 years	159	26%
11–15 years	118	19%
16–20 years	109	18%
>20 years	94	15%

sector SMEs from 09 districts of Pakistan collected through a close-ended questionnaire in 2019 as a part of a project. The data was collected from six major industries: food, textile, leather, sports, metal, and furniture. Table 7.3 shows the respondent firms' demography and Table 7.4 exhibits the respondent employees demography.

7.5.2 Measurement

The construct of attitude, attributes, absorptive capacity, and innovation was adopted from the study of Mubarik (2015). The attitude and attribute are second-order constructs, each with 05 sub-constructs and with 11 items and 21 items, respectively. The innovation had a first-order construct with 07 items. The construct of absorptive capacity was adopted from Flatten *et al.* (2011), which has two sub-constructs, namely realized absorptive capacity and potential absorptive capacity, with 14 items. All the items were gauged on the Likert scale of 05, 01 for strongly disagree to 05 for strongly agree. Table 7.5 summarizes the constructs, sub-constructs, items, and the supporting literature for each construct.

7.5.3 Method

We have employed Partial least square-structural equation modeling (PLS-SEM) for analyzing the hypothesized relationships. PLS-SEM is employed in two steps.

Beyond Conventional Human Capital 89

Table 7.4 Respondent Employees Demography

	N = 614	%
Designation		
Director	7	1%
General Manager	19	3%
Dy General Manager	29	5%
Senior Manager	201	33%
Manager	247	40%
Dy Manager	111	18%
Experience		
6–10 years	110	18%
11–15 years	241	39%
16–20 years	179	29%
>20 years	84	14%

Table 7.5 Sources of Constructs and their Indicators

Construct(s)	Sub-construct(s)	Items	Source(s)
Absorptive Capacity	Potential Absorptive Capacity Realized Absorptive Capacity	14 items	Flatten et al. (2011)
Attitude	Satisfaction Motivation Co-operation Engagement Commitment	11 items	Mubarik (2015)
Attributes	Leadership Intelligence Risk-taking Diversity Creativity	21 items	Mubarik (2015)
Innovation		07 items	Mubarik (2015)

At the first step, the reliability and validity of the measurement model are ascertained. This is done by analyzing by ensuring the internal consistency, reliability, convergent validity, and discriminant validity of the measurement models/constructs. At the second stage, after ascertaining the validity and reliability of the measurement model, the structural model is analyzed to test the developed hypotheses.

7.6 Reliability and Validity of Measurement Model

The reliability of the constructs has been examined by checking the values of the factor loading, composite reliability (CR), and Cronbach alpha. The

90   *Beyond Conventional Human Capital*

results of Reliability tests, exhibited in Table 7.6, show that CR and CB alpha values are higher than the threshold value of 0.70. It confirms the reliability of the all the constructs. Further, the values of factor loadings float between 0.63 to 0.81, showing that all the items well load on their

Table 7.6 Constructs Reliability and Vailidty

Construct(s)	Sub-construct(s)	CB Alpha	CR	AVE	Indicator	Factor loading
Absorptive Capacity	Potential Absorptive Capacity	0.73	0.83	0.55	Acqu3	0.64
					Assim2	0.82
					Assim3	0.75
					Assim4	0.75
	Realized Absorptive Capacity	0.81	0.86	0.52	Expl1	0.80
					Expl2	0.81
					Expl3	0.68
Innovation		0.81	0.86	0.52	Inv1	0.44
					Inv2	0.80
					Inv3	0.79
					Inv5	0.67
					Inv6	0.78
					Inv7	0.79
Attitude	Satisfaction	0.69	0.86	0.76	Satis1	0.87
					Satis2	0.87
	Motivation	0.63	0.84	0.73	Mot1	0.86
					Mot2	0.85
	Cooperation	0.65	0.85	0.74	Coop1	0.85
					Coop2	0.87
	Engagement	0.74	0.85	0.66	Eng1	0.81
					Eng2	0.81
					Eng3	0.81
	Commitment	0.64	0.85	0.74	Commit1	0.86
					Commit2	0.86
Attributes	Leadership	0.76	0.86	0.67	Lead1	0.86
					Lead2	0.83
					Lead3	0.78
	Intelligence	0.74	0.85	0.66	Int1	0.83
					Int2	0.81
					Int3	0.80
	Risk Taking	0.67	0.86	0.75	RT1	0.87
					RT2	0.87
	Diversity	0.81	0.87	0.63	Div1	0.78
					Div2	0.79
					Div3	0.81
					Div4	0.80
	Creativity	0.71	0.84	0.63	Creat1	0.78
					Creat2	0.77
					Creat3	0.83

Note: *Threshold value of AVE, CR, and CB alpha are 0.50, 0.60 and 0.70 respectively.*

respective constructs. Although the value of item $Inv1$ is 0.44, which is less than the recommended value of 0.60, we have retained it in the construct as its deletion does not improve AVE of the Construct (Hair et al. 2016). The validity of the constructs has been ascertained from both aspects of convergent validity and discriminant avidity. The AVE values of all constructs are higher than 0.50, clearly indicating the convergent validity of the constructs. For examining the discriminant validity, Fornell-Larcker criteria have been adopted (Fornell and Larcker 1994). As shown in Table 7.7, the diagonal values are square rooted values of AVE, which are higher than inter-construct correlation, showing the discriminant validity of all constructs. These results confirm the reliability and validity of the measurement models and allow to proceed for structural model analysis.

7.7 Results and Discussion

Table 7.8 shows the results of the path analysis for the overall sample, which indicates a few interesting observations. Firstly, we found evidence that Attitude (β = 0.194; t-value = 4.042) and Attributes (β = 0.159; t-$value$ = 3.118) to have direct impact on both the absorptive capacity at 1% significant level. It suggests that building absorptive capacity requires managers to look beyond conventional human capital, considering attitude and personal attributes matters. Likewise, the results support effect of attitude (β = 0.16; t-$value$ = 2.222) and personal attributes (β = 0.25; t-$value$ = 6.25) on absorptive capacity were also found significant. Contrastingly, the results do not support the mediating role of absorptive capacity in the association between attitude and innovation (β = 0.062; t-$value$ = 1.248). However, the results support the mediating role of absorptive capacity in the relationship between attributes and innovation (β = 0.098; t-$value$ = 8.864). It suggests that both knowledge acquisition, assimilation, and exploitation should occur jointly to mediate the relationship between attitude, attributes, and innovation. Likewise, all the individual effects of attitudes and attributes are significant. The results of the impact of overall behavioural capital on innovation, directly and through absorptive capacity, support both hypotheses of the study and validate the proposed model.

The results overwhelmingly support the proposed model of the study and highlight the momentous role of behavioural human capital in innovation (See Table 7.9). Comparing the findings of the study with the extant literature, we find that our study is echoing the same notion which has been thinly discussed in the literature. For example, the McGuirk et al. (2015), Mollick (2012) and Mubarik (2015) argue that behavioural aspects of human capital can exert a positive impact on the innovation performance of a firm. This study explains how behavioural human capital can influence a firm's innovation and absorptive capacity and presents empirical evidence to support this association. Hence, our study helps understand the findings of previous studies where the role of attitude and attributes was mentioned as important for innovation, but its transmission mechanism was not illustrated.

Table 7.7 Fornell-Larcker Criteria

	AC-P	AC-R	Commit	Coop	Creat	Div	Eng	Inv	Int	Lead	Mot	RT	Satis
AC-P	*0.743*												
AC-R	0.486	*0.719*											
Commit	0.104	0.132	*0.858*										
Coop	0.133	0.148	0.717	*0.862*									
Creat	0.156	0.197	0.059	0.049	*0.794*								
Div	0.111	0.192	0.088	0.092	0.745	*0.794*							
Eng	0.079	0.134	0.565	0.503	0.062	0.077	*0.81*						
Inv	0.155	0.16	0.081	0.065	0.077	0.067	0.047	*0.722*					
Int	0.098	0.172	0.062	0.046	0.579	0.691	0.035	0.12	*0.812*				
Lead	0.125	0.136	0.028	0.033	0.505	0.554	0.051	0.096	0.625	*0.82*			
Mot	0.128	0.08	0.615	0.508	0.109	0.072	0.655	0.135	0.086	0.029	*0.854*		
RT	0.099	0.207	0.098	0.077	0.603	0.699	0.051	0.10	0.71	0.581	0.081	*0.868*	
Satis	0.101	0.115	0.677	0.57	0.049	0.018	0.62	0.16	0.10	0.031	0.713	0.084	*0.872*

Note: The diagonal values are square rooted AVE.

Beyond Conventional Human Capital   93

Table 7.8 Path Analysis

Path	β	SE	t-Val
Attitudes → Innovation	0.194	0.048	4.042**
Attributes → Innovation	0.159	0.051	3.118**
Attitudes → Absorptive Capacity	0.160	0.072	2.222**
Attributes →Absorptive Capacity	0.250	0.040	6.250*
Absorptive Capacity → Innovation	0.390	0.089	4.382**
Attitudes → Absorptive Capacity → Innovation	0.062	0.050	1.248
Attributes → Absorptive Capacity →Innovation	0.098	0.011	8.864***

Note: *R-Square 0.54, Q-Square 0.27.*
*** and *** show the level of significance at 5% and 1%.*

Table 7.9 Hypotheses Testing

Hypothesis	Beta	SE	t-value	Decision
behavioural HC → Innovation	0.287	0.067	4.284**	Supported
behavioural HC → Absorptive Capacity → Innovation	0.111	0.042	2.665**	Supported

7.8 Concluding Remarks

This study explains the notion of behavioural human capital and presents a framework modeling the impact of BHC on a firm's absorptive capacity and innovation performance. The study tests the proposed framework by taking the data from the SMEs of Pakistan. The empirical investigation supports the derived framework, highlighting the significant role of BHC in improving innovation directly and through absorptive capacity. Our results may not be groundbreaking from the perspective of finding any new antecedent of innovation. Still, these results allow us to relook at the importance of behavioural human capital while devising the organizational human capital development strategy. This study has contributed to the integration of the dispersed literature on the role of attitude and attributes in building the firm's absorptive capacity and innovation and offering it in the form of a testable framework.

We would suggest future researchers examine the applicability of the proposed framework by conducting empirical studies in various settings, e.g., cross country, cross industry, etc.

References

Adegoke, O., Gerard, B., & Andrew, M. (2007). Innovation types and performance in growing UK SMEs. *International Journal of Operations & Production Management*, 27(7), 735–753.

Beyond Conventional Human Capital

Ahmed, S. S., Guozhu, J., Mubarik, S., Khan, M., & Khan, E. (2020). Intellectual capital and business performance: The role of dimensions of absorptive capacity. *Journal of Intellectual Capital*, 21(1), 23–39.

Ahmed, S. S., Khan, M. M., Khan, E., Sohail, F., & Mahmood, N. (2021). Enhancing intellectual capital and organizational performance through talent management. In *The Dynamics of Intellectual Capital in Current Era* (pp. 205–220). Springer, Singapore.

Allameh, S. M., Shahriari, M., & Mansoori, H. (2012). Investigating employee's attitude toward organization, organizational climate and employee's engagement as antecedents of organizational citizenship behavior. *Australian Journal of Basic and Applied Sciences*, 6(8), 384–393.

Armstrong, M. (2006) *A Handbook of Human Resource Management Practice* (10 ed.), Kogan Books, United Kingdom

Bonesso, S., Gerli, F., Pizzi, C., & Boyatzis, R. E. (2020). The role of intangible human capital in innovation diversification: Linking behavioral competencies with different types of innovation. *Industrial and Corporate Change*, 29(3), 661–681.

Bartoloni, E., & Baussola, M. (2016). Does technological innovation undertaken alone have a real pivotal role? Product and marketing innovation in manufacturing firms. *Economics of Innovation and New Technology*, 25(2), 91–113.

Becker, T. E., Billings, R. S., Eveleth, D. M., & Gilbert, N. L. (1996). Foci and bases of employee commitment: Implications for job performance. *Academy of management journal*, 39(2), 464–482.

Chamadia, S., & Mubarik, M. S. (2021). Assessing the effectiveness of vocational training programs in Pakistan: An experimental study. *Education+ Training*. 63(5), 665–678.

Cohen, W. M., & Levinthal, D. A. (1990). Absorptive capacity: A new perspective on learning and innovation. *Administrative science quarterly*, 35(1), 128–152.

Cascio, W. F. (2010). *Managing Human Resources: Productivity, Quality of Work, Profits*. McGraw Hill, United States.

Christensen, C. M., Marx, M., & Stevenson, H. H. (2006). The tools of cooperation and change. *Harvard Business Review*, 84(10), 72–87.

Chemers, M. M. (2000). Leadership research and theory: A functional integration. *Group Dynamics: Theory, Research, and Practice*, 4(1), 27–38.

Dodgson, M. (1993). Organizational learning: A review of some literatures. *Organization studies*, 14(3), 375–394.

Flatten, T. C., Greve, G. I., & Brettel, M. (2011). Absorptive capacity and firm performance in SMEs: The mediating influence of strategic alliances. *European Management Review*, 8(3), 137–152.

Fornell, C., and Larcker, D. F. (1994). Evaluating structural equation models with unobservable variables and measurement error, *Journal Marketing Research*, 18, 29–50.

Hair Jr, J. F., Hult, G. T. M., Ringle, C., & Sarstedt, M. (2016). *A Primer On Partial Least Squares Structural Equation Modeling (PLS-SEM)*. Sage publications.

Kular, S., Gatenby, M., Rees, C., Soane, E., & Truss, K. (2008). *Employee Engagement: A Literature Review: Kingston Business School*. Kingston University.

Kusi-Sarpong, S., Mubarik, M. S., Khan, S. A., Brown, S., & Mubarak, M. F. (2022). Intellectual capital, blockchain-driven supply chain and sustainable production: Role of supply chain mapping. *Technological Forecasting and Social Change*, 175, 121331.

Lane, P. J., & Lubatkin, M. (1998). Relative absorptive capacity and interorganizational learning. *Strategic management journal*, 19(5), 461–477.

Madjar, N. (2005). The contributions of different groups of individuals to employees' creativity. *Advances in Developing Human Resources*, 7(2), 182–206.

Mahmood, T., & Mubarik, M. S. (2020). Balancing innovation and exploitation in the fourth industrial revolution: Role of intellectual capital and technology absorptive capacity. *Technological Forecasting and Social Change*, 160, 120248.

Massa, S., & Testa, S. (2008). Innovation and SMEs: Misaligned perspectives and goals among entrepreneurs, academics, and policy makers. *Technovation*, 28(7), 393–407.

McGuirk, H., & Jordan, D. (2012). Local labour market diversity and business innovation: Evidence from Irish manufacturing businesses. *European Planning Studies*, 20(12), 1945–1960.

McGuirk, H., Lenihan, H., & Hart, M. (2015). Measuring the impact of innovative human capital on small firms' propensity to innovate. *Research Policy*, 44(4), 965–976.

Mollick, E. (2012). People and process, suits and innovators: The role of individuals in firm performance. *Strategic Management Journal*, 33(9), 1001–1015.

Mowday, R. T., Porter, L. W., & Steers, R. M. (2013). *Employee—organization linkages: The psychology of commitment, absenteeism, and turnover*. Academic press.

Mubarik, M. S. (2015). *Human Capital and Performance of Small & Medium Manufacturing Enterprises: A Study of Pakistan* (Doctoral dissertation, University of Malaya). Accessed from: http://studentsrepo.um.edu.my/6573/ (24 February 2020).

Mubarik, M. S., Chandran, V. G. R., & Devadason, E. S. (2018). Measuring human capital in small and medium manufacturing enterprises: What matters?. *Social Indicators Research*, 137(2), 605–623.

Mubarik, M. S., Devadason, E. S., & Govindaraju, C. (2020). Human capital and export performance of small and medium enterprises in Pakistan. *International Journal of Social Economics*, 47(5), 643–662.

Mubarik, M. S., Bontis, N., Mubarik, M., & Mahmood, T. (2021). Intellectual capital and supply chain resilience. *Journal of Intellectual Capital*. Ahead of print. 10.1108/JIC-06-2020-0206

Pradana, M., Pérez-Luño, A., & Fuentes-Blasco, M. (2020). Innovation as the key to gain performance from absorptive capacity and human capital. *Technology Analysis & Strategic Management*, 32(7), 822–834.

Rainlall, S. (2004). A review of employee motivation theories and their implications for employee retention within organizations. *The Journal of American Academy of Business*, 9(1), 21–26.

Robbins, T. W., & Everitt, B. J. (1996). Neurobehavioural mechanisms of reward and motivation. *Current Opinion in Neurobiology*, 6(2), 228–236.

Saari, L. M., & Judge, T. A. (2004). Employee attitudes and job satisfaction. *Human Resource Management: Published in Cooperation with the School of Business Administration, The University of Michigan and in alliance with the Society of Human Resources Management*, 43(4), 395–407.

Schumpeter, J. (1942). Creative destruction. *Capitalism, socialism and democracy*, 825, 82–85.

Van Saane, N., Sluiter, J., Verbeek, J., & Frings-Dresen, M. (2003). Reliability and validity of instruments measuring job satisfaction—A systematic review. *Occupational Medicine*, 53(3), 191–200.

Wernerfelt, B. (1984). A resource-based view of the firm. *Strategic management journal*, 5(2), 171–180.

Zahra, S. A., & George, G. (2002). Absorptive capacity: A review, reconceptualization, and extension. *Academy of management review*, 27(2), 185–203.

Appendix A Cross-loadings

	AC-P	AC-R	Commit	Coop	Creat	Div	Eng	Inv	Int	Lead	Mot	RT	Satis
Acqu3	0.641	0.302	0.048	0.099	0.112	0.084	0.05	0.079	0.047	0.027	0.092	0.052	0.051
Assim2	0.82	0.391	0.093	0.094	0.163	0.1	0.105	0.135	0.09	0.147	0.11	0.072	0.069
Assim3	0.749	0.427	0.06	0.111	0.09	0.055	-0.022	0.135	0.103	0.069	0.068	0.086	0.108
Assim4	0.752	0.32	0.099	0.096	0.091	0.089	0.091	0.102	0.043	0.103	0.11	0.082	0.069
Commit1	0.138	0.147	0.858	0.669	0.047	0.083	0.468	0.053	0.054	0.016	0.51	0.09	0.568
Commit2	0.039	0.081	0.858	0.561	0.055	0.068	0.503	0.086	0.052	0.032	0.546	0.078	0.594
Coop1	0.105	0.112	0.543	0.852	0.104	0.136	0.449	0.039	0.081	0.056	0.43	0.127	0.468
Coop2	0.124	0.142	0.688	0.872	-0.015	0.027	0.42	0.072	0.001	0.003	0.446	0.011	0.513
Creat1	0.049	0.152	0.026	-0.01	0.783	0.563	0.028	0.03	0.408	0.345	0.09	0.447	0.027
Creat2	0.184	0.15	0.055	0.032	0.77	0.57	0.07	0.154	0.495	0.439	0.141	0.462	0.068
Creat3	0.132	0.165	0.058	0.089	0.827	0.638	0.049	0.002	0.473	0.414	0.032	0.523	0.021
Div1	0.126	0.159	0.047	0.072	0.61	0.777	0.031	0.081	0.525	0.432	0.042	0.518	-0.002
Div2	0.066	0.066	0.089	0.03	0.577	0.792	0.089	-0.031	0.53	0.451	0.044	0.569	-0.005
Div3	0.105	0.227	0.096	0.087	0.621	0.808	0.074	0.065	0.575	0.465	0.071	0.556	0.046
Div4	0.054	0.154	0.046	0.104	0.558	0.8	0.051	0.098	0.565	0.411	0.073	0.579	0.019
Eng1	0.151	0.164	0.495	0.465	0.044	0.027	0.814	0.148	0.016	0.022	0.528	0.055	0.534
Eng2	0.09	0.107	0.418	0.337	0.086	0.115	0.807	-0.064	0.073	-0.005	0.567	0.053	0.481
Eng3	-0.054	0.051	0.458	0.415	0.022	0.05	0.809	0.021	-0.003	-0.018	0.496	0.016	0.488
Expl1	0.358	0.797	0.135	0.085	0.15	0.146	0.163	0.16	0.156	0.073	0.103	0.149	0.116
Expl2	0.282	0.805	0.068	0.092	0.113	0.164	0.119	0.137	0.162	0.151	0.003	0.178	0.079
Expl3	0.301	0.68	0.108	0.119	0.088	0.059	0.086	0.096	0.061	0.091	0.03	0.128	0.085
Int1	0.073	0.16	0.072	0.043	0.475	0.554	0.023	0.093	0.825	0.49	0.068	0.585	0.106
Int2	0.088	0.133	0.054	0.059	0.492	0.619	0.033	0.086	0.813	0.515	0.087	0.586	0.079
Int3	0.077	0.125	0.024	0.008	0.443	0.507	0.028	0.114	0.798	0.517	0.053	0.533	0.058
Inv1	0.149	0.133	0.172	0.12	0.016	-0.024	0.058	0.435	0	-0.004	0.136	0.031	0.113
Inv2	0.09	0.071	0.044	0.038	0.093	0.073	0.021	0.802	0.151	0.158	0.087	0.108	0.115

Inv3	0.076	0.121	−0.017	−0.007	0.073	0.046	0.013	0.788	0.143	0.118	0.043	0.084	0.099
Inv5	0.067	0.076	−0.042	−0.015	0.044	0.037	−0.069	0.671	0.046	0.036	0	0.014	0.014
Inv6	0.11	0.125	0.061	0.061	−0.004	0.034	0.039	0.776	0.053	0.008	0.104	0.034	0.126
Inv7	0.124	0.121	0.039	0.026	0.1	0.112	0.063	0.79	0.11	0.09	0.125	0.12	0.145
Lead1	0.127	0.177	0.066	0.094	0.423	0.512	0.068	0.059	0.555	0.856	0.03	0.534	0.047
Lead2	0.108	0.135	0.004	−0.012	0.413	0.442	−0.079	0.067	0.523	0.828	0.003	0.479	0.01
Lead3	0.067	0.01	−0.008	−0.009	0.406	0.404	0.008	0.116	0.454	0.776	0.04	0.409	0.018
Mot1	0.078	0.048	0.537	0.455	0.083	0.068	0.529	0.125	0.057	0.079	0.857	0.081	0.645
Mot1	0.078	0.048	0.537	0.455	0.083	0.068	0.529	0.125	0.057	0.079	0.857	0.081	0.645
Mot2	0.141	0.09	0.514	0.412	0.104	0.055	0.59	0.106	0.09	−0.03	0.851	0.057	0.571
Mot2	0.141	0.09	0.514	0.412	0.104	0.055	0.59	0.106	0.09	−0.03	0.851	0.057	0.571
RT1	0.12	0.177	0.075	0.064	0.537	0.619	0.059	0.114	0.615	0.499	0.062	0.871	0.064
RT2	0.051	0.182	0.096	0.071	0.51	0.594	0.03	0.059	0.6	0.51	0.079	0.865	0.081
Satis1	0.064	0.11	0.577	0.494	0.036	0.019	0.525	0.179	0.077	0.031	0.633	0.102	0.87
Satis2	0.111	0.091	0.603	0.501	0.049	0.013	0.555	0.101	0.098	0.023	0.61	0.044	0.874
Trans1	0.491	0.651	0.081	0.135	0.171	0.15	0.086	0.119	0.145	0.152	0.089	0.177	0.079
Trans3	0.346	0.658	0.05	0.076	0.155	0.16	0.021	0.072	0.08	0.075	−0.014	0.107	−0.027
Trans4	0.304	0.706	0.121	0.137	0.17	0.137	0.061	0.074	0.098	0.023	0.106	0.132	0.134

VIF

Indicators	VIF	Indicator	VIF	Indicators	VIF	Indicators	VIF
Acqu3	1.266	Commit2	1.852	Creat2	1.3	Div2	1.846
Assim2	1.517	Coop1	1.309	Creat2	1.64	Div3	1.674
Assim3	1.403	Coop1	1.553	Creat3	1.476	Div3	2.013
Assim4	1.425	Coop2	1.309	Creat3	1.859	Div4	1.661
Commit1	1.289	Coop2	2.075	Div1	1.558	Div4	1.915
Commit1	2.151	Creat1	1.411	Div1	1.824	Eng1	1.434
Commit2	1.289	Creat1	1.609	Div2	1.628	Eng1	1.728
Eng2	1.481	Int1	1.538	Inv2	2.2	Lead2	1.579
Eng2	1.781	Int1	1.819	Inv3	2.247	Lead2	1.738
Eng3	1.475	Int2	1.44	Inv5	1.795	Lead3	1.414
Eng3	1.65	Int2	1.903	Inv6	1.928	Lead3	1.564
Expl1	1.84	Int3	1.462	Inv7	1.909	Mot1	1.267
Expl2	1.973	Int3	1.695	Lead1	1.658	Mot1	1.91
Expl3	1.599	Inv1	1.056	Lead1	1.913	Mot2	1.267
Mot2	1.87	Satis2	1.373	Satis1	1.373		
RT1	1.346	Satis2	1.937	Satis1	2.009		
RT1	1.943	Trans1	1.402				
RT2	1.346	Trans3	1.541				
RT2	1.822	Trans4	1.518				

8 Human Capital in Cross-border Mergers and Acquisitions: An Exaptation Perspective

8.1 Introduction

A vast amount of literature could be found studying the role of the headquarters' location in the home country and its linkages with market forces and market structure (Beugelsdijk & Mudambi 2013). It is argued that firms with geographically dispersed business units perform better in cross-border activities than others. A significant stream of literature, which can help explain why some firms, having geographically dispersed units in the home country, can perform better than others, is the exaptation of human capital (HC). Drawing on Santangelo and Stucchi (2018) study, we argue that domestically dispersed business units develop a firm's specific human capital—the human capital capability of control and coordination—which can be reutilized in cross-border mergers acquisition. The literature on the role of exaptive human capital (EHC) is scant, and only a few studies can be found in this context. These studies stress the need for research on the home country's influence on cross-border activities, especially cross-border mergers and acquisitions (CBMA). Santangelo and Stucchi (2018) study is the pioneering and perhaps the only study to the best of our knowledge, examining the role of exaptation in internationalization. Against this backdrop, this study introduces the notion EHC and argues that a firm's domestic geographical dispersion can help build a specific kind of human capital resource (HCR), which can positively contribute to its cross-border activities, especially mergers and acquisitions. We also propose that the impact of EHC, developed through home country geographical dispersion, is different in a firm's first and subsequent cross-border mergers and acquisitions or the same.

This study hypothesizes that firms operating their business units in dispersed geographical locations in host country improve their human capital resource by coordinating and managing nationally dispersed business units and can reutilize it in CBMAs (Beugelsdijk et al. 2010: Marquis & Huang 2010; Santangelo & Stucchi 2018). It is worth mentioning that these HC capabilities may lose their influence and relevance in the subsequent CBM&As (Santangelo & Stuchi 2018). This re-use of control and coordination capabilities (HC), attained domestically for a specific purpose, in

DOI: 10.4324/9781003195894-8

the process of CBM&A is termed as exaptation of human capital or exaptive human capital (EHC). The process of exaptation has been well described by the biologist working on the evolution of life. However, it has also been applied in evolution and management sciences economics. Santangelo and Stuchi (2018) have first used this term in international business theory and suggested future studies to extend this concept by investigating its relevance in other countries. Ching (2016, p. 182), defining exaptation, denotes, *"Exaptive features are typically produced by natural selection for a function other than the one it currently performs, which is then co-opted by the new function. In the management literature, the same term often refers to the exploitation of an existing body of knowledge so as to gain a competitive advantage in an emerging industry"*. This study develops the understanding of the exaptation by providing its linkages with CBMA. The study also examines the significance of domestic geography in internalization.

8.2 Literature Review

Although the application of the notion exaptation is very recent and limited in international business, it could be widely seen in other business management fields, e.g., entrepreneurship and innovation. For example, Cattani (2005, 2006) argued that exaptive processes directly contribute to the firm's competitive advantage. Describing the case of a leading fiber optics company, Corning, he explicitly explained as to how the company's market power was due to its exaptive abilities—*the abilities that Corning developed even before the inception of the industry in which it operates now"*. Ching (2016, p. 183), referring to Cattani (2005), construe, "The author shows that Corning's success results at least in part from their foresight in developing capabilities that they could "recycle" even as they expanded into new domains".

The proceeding section explains how the exaptation theory and human capital theory provide the theoretical foundations to our argument.

8.2.1 Theoretical Exposition

Operating in other countries poses significantly different and new challenges to the firm. These challenges could be different due to culture, geography, institutions, and distances (Hymer 1976). Studies (e.g., Ahmed et al. 2019; Clarke et al. 2012; Mubarik et al. 2020) highlight the importance of firm's relevant human capital ability while expanding abroad. Drawing from HC theory and RBV, developing human capital acts as the basis of critical organizational capacities required for a firm to successfully acquire and align external resources (Bird & Mendenhall 2016; Johanson & Vahlne 1977; Mahmood & Mubarik 2020; Mubarik & Naghavi 2020). In cross-border mergers and acquisitions, such capabilities are even more critical where a firm must deal with two major challenges, i.e., corporate culture difference and country difference (Barkema et al. 1996; Collins et al. 2009; Mubarik et al. 2021). Santangelo and Stuchi (2018) name these two challenges as "double-layered acculturation". While negotiating cross-border mergers and acquisitions, the firm must have stronger human capital resources competent enough to have an in-depth understanding of foreign country's complexities, e.g., exchange rate fluctuations, systems, culture, and respond accordingly—*strong human capital* (Reza et al. 2021).

Similarly, firms must possess the ability to develop a professional relationship with the various stakeholders in the host country environment. In short, HCR appears to be a critical competency required to undertake CBMA. Since HCR is greatly intangible and cannot be fully acquired externally, firms are required to develop these capabilities internally to successfully execute this process (Mubarik et al. 2020). Especially while engaging in the first CBMA, organizations have limited capabilities to acquire and integrate external resources. Some of the factors can help firm to overcome this issue. For example, firms develop human capital from external sources by hiring managers with international experience externally to overcome this limitation; however, it may not fill the capacity gap. A firm's previous experience in greenfield investment can assists in international ventures. However, according to Vermeulen and Barkema (2001), greenfield investment experience may not be instrumental in the process of CBMA as it may increase firms' rigidity towards CBMA. Likewise, the firm's prior experience in the joint venture is useful only in managing the relationship with partners. Further, the firm's acquisition experience in the domestic country may not be helpful as the complexity in international deals is much higher than domestic. Further, the firm must have an intact and well-integrated process for cross-border communication and coordination.

In this context, the firm can take great advantage of the HC capabilities and capacities developed to cater to domestically dispersed locations while engaging (Ahmed et al., 2019). This re-utilization of human capital capabilities, attained domestically in the internationalization process is called exaptation of human capital. The concept of exaptation is rooted in the field of evolutionary biology. Biologists explain exaptation as the re-utilization of capabilities acquired in a particular environment for a specific purpose in a different environment and different purposes (Aaltonen et al. 2020; Gould & Vrba 1982). For example, flight feathers have been exapted from decor feathers and thermal insulation. Similarly, floating swim bladders were exapted to breathing swim bladders (Santalego & Stucchi 2018). These capabilities were earlier developed to perform a particular function (adaptation) and then were reutilized (exapted) in a new situation. For Beltagui et al. (2020, p. 48), "The term exaptation was proposed by evolutionary biologists as a complement to adaptation. Whereas adaptation refers to features that develop for a specific function, such as larger lungs among Andean mountain people, exaptation refers to features that are later found to be useful for unintended functions".

102 An Exaptation Perspective

In management research, the notion exaptation urges that a firm can reutilize (exapt) the capabilities in a different environment, which were acquired initially for responding to a specific environment (Marquis & Huang 2010). Put it simply, exaptation denotes a state where the current application of a capability is different than its historical origin (Aaltonen 2020; Winter & Szulanski 2001). Santangelo and Stuchi (2018) explained the concept of exaptation in context of internationalization, suggesting that firms involved in first-time CBMAs exapt (reutilize) capabilities of management, coordination, and control. This includes firms' capabilities to communicate, socialize, process information, and select and standardize best business practices. These capabilities form the intellectual capital of a firm. To reduce coordination transaction costs in domestically dispersed units, firms develop such HCR. These costs have a direct relationship with the extent of geographical dispersion. The more a firm's business units are located at distances from each other, the more will be the difficulties in coordinating and aligning incentives (Jones & Hill 1988; Cheng et al. 2017). To control such costs, firms develop standard procedures for arranging meetings on time, traveling, and virtual teams. Firms also develop information systems that help an agile and effective exchange and monitoring of information. Likewise, firms develop standardized processes for aligning internal procedures with shared best practices. It is important to note that geographically dispersed units may not be linked with market saturation or dominance. These units are different than business selling units, and it is possible that a firm can saturate the domestic market even without dispersing them geographically. Likewise, greater geographical dispersion may not represent market dominance as different domestically dispersed organizational units may operate in different market segments.

8.2.2 Hypothesis Development

The question of the cost and benefits of economic activities in a geographically dispersed environment has been long debated by the researcher of economic geography. Although there is a large debate on the extent of cost and benefits of domestic geography, all researchers agree that an organization working in geographically dispersed units has to control its cost and take advantage by connecting dispersed locations across distances (Beugelsdijk et al. 2010; Hendriks 2020). While operating in the domestically dispersed domestic environment, firms require to develop and standardize strong remote management processes for effectively managing, coordinating, and monitoring their home country operations, further enhancing intra-organizational coordination and information sharing (Wang et al. 2020).

The span of such activity needs to be expanded to various business activities along the value chains to reap the benefit of cross activity links (Mudambi 2008; Nachum & Zaheer 2005; Aaltonen 202). Further, comparing geographically dispersed firms with those geographically concentrated firms, the former confronts comparatively higher transaction costs. Therefore, geographically dispersed firms require to develop the spatial HC capabilities of coordination and control. Although the degree of effectiveness of such capabilities can differ by organization, the firms operating in the geographically dispersed environment may surpass their geographically concentrated counterparts if any opportunity to exapt (reutilize) such capabilities appears (Hendriks 2020). For example, while CBMA is in the pre-acquisition phase, the firm's procedures developed to organize meetings and arrange visits can be re-used (exapt) in organizing the auditors' travels for evaluating the possible target(s), planning required action for acquisition, understanding regulations and value systems, and to control the potential international impediments.

Similarly, in the post-acquisition process, such domestically developed processes and standards can be re-applied (exapted) for forming integration teams for planning, managing, and executing the process of integration and learning the peculiarities of the targeted context to operate productively. At this stage, the information systems built to cater to the domestically dispersed business units can also be re-deployed in CBMA to control decision-making. Further, during this stage, capacities obtained previously for aligning processes and routines of home-country dispersed units can be effectively reused. This re-deployment can help identify the mature and established processes at the target firm for competing for the peculiarities of host-country context and further synchronize these processes with the internal processes. Firms built the IC capabilities for a purpose other than CBMA (Wang & Kafouros 2020). These HC capabilities and capacities are first built to respond to operations' domestic geographical dispersion as an adaptive process. The re-deployment of these HC capacities and capabilities in the international context for engaging and managing cross-border mergers and acquisitions is exaptation (Dew et al. 2004; Wang et al. 2020). By keeping in view the earlier observations, we draw our first hypothesis:

Hypothesis 1. There exists a positive relationship between a firm's EHC, developed through domestic geographical dispersion, and chances to engage in first-time CBMA.

After the first CBMA, the firm tends to develop new HC capabilities and capacities related to the new environment and context. These newly developed HC capabilties may supersede the firm's exapted capabilities (Andriani & Kaminska 2021; Gould 1991). For example, the capabilities of control and coordination accrued from the domestic environment and re-deployed in the first time CBMA may lose their importance in the subsequent CBMA as the organization has already developed the new capabilities specific to the international environment. The use of newly developed capabilities is more effective than re-using the old capabilities as the newly developed capabilities are

104 *An Exaptation Perspective*

more relevant and have higher potential to give leverage to the firm to compete in an international environment (Nelson & Winter 2002; Vahlne & Johanson 2017). In a nutshell, the domestically developed capacities of control and coordination help a firm complete the challenge of "double-layered acculturation" effectively in the first CBMA. However, in subsequent CBMA, due to the newly developed capabilities, the exapted capabilities may become less critical comparatively. Therefore, domestic geographic dispersion is higher on the probability that a firm involves first-time CBMA than the subsequent CBMA. Against this backdrop, we hypothesize:

Hypothesis 2. Effect of a firm's EHC, developed through domestic geographical dispersion, is higher on the chances of its first CBMA as compared to its subsequent CBMA.

8.3 Model

Previous discussion allows us to draw the following testable model.

$$CBMA = \alpha + \beta_1 DGD + \beta_2 ENT + \beta_3 XEXP + \beta_4 JVEX + \beta_5 DAE + \beta_6 DMS$$
$$+ \beta_7 INTG + \beta_8 INDD + \beta_9 PROF + \beta_{10} SIZE + \beta_{11} AGE$$
$$+ \phi \dots \dots \dots \dots \dots \dots \dots \tag{8.1}$$

Whereas, ENT represents an entry. It can be calculated by following the procedure described by Santangelo and Stuchi (2018). According to Santangelo and Stucchi (2018), to consider firms' location decisions, preliminary to the hurdle, a mixed logit model is to be estimated to calculate the maximum predicted value for each firm year to include this variable (entry) in the hurdle.

Acronym DGD represents domestic geographical dispersion. Studies e.g., Santangelo and Stuchi (2018), domestic geographical dispersion have been measured using the postcode (i.e., distance from headquarters to units) of each firm, with a year lag of a rescaled Hirschman–Herfindahl index (HHI). If the value of DGD is closer to 01, the firm has many dispersed business units in many divisions, and if its value is 0, it has one unit in one division.

In addition to the aforementioned primary variables, we also suggest introducing the following control variables:

- XEXP represents the previous experience of internationalization, measured by export intensity;
- JVEX describes joint venture experience measured as the total number of joint ventures;

- DAE is a domestic acquisition experience measured in the first step as the log of the total number of domestic acquisitions;
- DMS is a domestic market share measured as the share of sales over total sale;
- INT are intangibles value measured by the advertising-to-sales ratio (intangibles);
- INDD is industrial diversification, we have taken the rescaled value of HHI calculated across the manufacturing sector to measure it;
- PROF is profitability gauged by operating profits.
- SIZE is firm size measured as the log of the total number of employees;
- AGE is the age of the firm measured by the number of years since incorporation.

8.4 Discussions

The study highlights that a firm's specific human capital capabilities attained in the domestic environment may not necessarily be re-employed for the same task. However, such capabilities could be instrumental in performing or supporting some altogether different yet important tasks. It highlights that human capital developed in a particular context may not outrightly be rejected and must be examined in detail to determine as to how it can be relevant in the different context. In short, the study integrates the literature from human capital and internationalization and offers a theoretical framework to understand the performance difference of the firm embarking on CBMA.

Based on the model of this study, we draw some important insights. First is the top and middle-level management's orientation regarding the role of specific HCR capabilities—*developed for some particular purpose or under a particular environment*—in strategic ventures other than for which these were originally developed. The majority of the managers focus on developing or acquiring HCR for any new or different strategic venture without realizing the use of existing HCR in that particular context. One of the major reasons for it is bounded orientation on the usage of these resources. Most of the managers do not look beyond the traditional use of HCR and always try to focus on the acquisition or development of new resources rather than reutilizing (exapting) the existing ones. Our model indicates that managers must re-utilize existing HCR capabilities in the new and different ventures. We argue that organizations should systematically promote the thinking of and use of exaptations at each level of organizational hierarchy. Promoting such thinking can help organizations systematically adopt the expatation as a unique competitive strategy.

Scholars differ on whether exaptation is a deliberate process or instant recognition of an organizational resource that can be used for other important purposes. Without negating the possibility of instantaneous recognition, we argue that exaptation can be a deliberate process and can be

106 *An Exaptation Perspective*

developed through a well-thought strategy. It is essential to note that exaptation differs from invention and discovery. As mentioned by Andriani and Kaminska (2021, p. 2), "exaptation differs from the process of invention and discovery but shares with them some common features. It differs from invention because exaptation is 'found' not 'made'. It is also different from discovery because exaptation concerns the co-option of an existing artifact for a new function (although the new function could be discovered)".

8.5 Concluding Remarks

This study extends the understanding of exaptation one step further, following the footprints of Santangelo and Stuchi (2018). We introduce the concept of exapitve human capital (EHC), building upon Santangelo and Stuchi (2018) study, which argues that firms having geographically dispersed domestic business units develop capabilities of control and coordination for managing the domestic business units. The firm reuses these capabilities and capacities while engaging in cross-border mergers and acquisitions. This study explicates it as the "exaptation of human capital", the re-utilization of HCR capabilities and features first acquired for a particular purpose in a particular context to an entirely different context and purpose. We propose that HCR capabilities of control and coordination have a positive and significant impact of first-time CBMA; however, these capabilities become irrelevant in subsequent CBMA involvements. Internationalization, especially CBMAs, faces many discontinue and hurdles due to the new international environment and random functional shifts. In this context, EHC provides firms' capabilities to control such discontinuities (Santangelo & Meyer 2017). Our study elucidates the role and relevance of domestic geographical dispersion in the early phases of CBMA.

We would suggest future research studies to empirically investigate this study's proposed model. Likewise, we also suggest future research to work on the exaptation of intellectual capital (EIC), which, along with human capital resources, can take into account relational capital and process capital as well. The proposed model of the study opens new avenues for future research. Based on the results, we argue that an organization's human capital resource can be used in different contexts to attain different performance outcomes. Our proposition is supported by Dew and Sarasvathy (2016 p. 167), who mentions, "exaptation draws our attention to the repurposing of artifacts, technologies, processes, skills, organizations, and resources for emergent uses that they were not designed for". These findings also highlight the need to relook at the IC based view of a firm in the context of internationalization. One question we pose to the scholars is to determine whether the concept of the exaptation is deterministic or ties with the Knightian uncertainty (serendipitous use). In the case of the former, the firms can capitalize on the exaptation by developing appropriate business strategies to seize any business opportunity or encounter threats. In the simplest sense, the exaptation-led strategy could be adopted to compete for the rival firms. However, in the case of the later, Knightian uncertainty, the concept of exaptation may be of limited use as the existence of uncertainty may not allow firms to fully capitalize on the exaptive capabilities. This confusion needs the attention of the scholars for its clarification.

References

Aaltonen, P. H. M. (2020). Piecing together a puzzle—A review and research agenda on internationalization and the promise of exaptation. *International Business Review*, 29(4), 101664.

Aaltonen, P., Torkkeli, L., & Worek, M. (2020). The effect of emerging economies operations on knowledge utilization: The behavior of international companies as exaptation and adaptation. In *International Business and Emerging Economy Firms* (pp. 49–87). Palgrave Macmillan, Cham.

Ahmed, S. S., Guozhu, J., Mubarik, S., Khan, M., & Khan, E. (2019). Intellectual capital and business performance: The role of dimensions of absorptive capacity. *Journal of Intellectual Capital*. 21(1), 23–39.

Andriani, P., & Kaminska, R. (2021). Exploring the dynamics of novelty production through exaptation: A historical analysis of coal tar-based innovations. *Research Policy*, 50(2), 104171.

Bae, K. H., Kang, J. K., & Kim, J. M. (2002). Tunneling or value added? Evidence from mergers by Korean business groups. *The Journal of Finance*, 57(6), 2695–2740.

Barkema, H. G., Bell, J. H., & Pennings, J. M. (1996). Foreign entry, cultural barriers, and learning. *Strategic Management Journal*, 17(2): 151–166.

Beltagui, A., Rosli, A., & Candi, M. (2020). Exaptation in a digital innovation ecosystem: The disruptive impacts of 3D printing. *Research policy*, 49(1), 103833.

Beugelsdijk, S., McCann, P., & Mudambi, R. (2010). Introduction: Place, space and organization—economic geography and the multinational enterprise. *Journal of Economic Geography*, 10(4), 485–493.

Beugelsdijk, S., & Mudambi, R. (2013). MNEs as border-crossing multi-location enterprises: The role of discontinuities in geographic space. *Journal of International Business Studies*, 44(5), 413–426.

Bird, A., & Mendenhall, M. E. (2016). From cross-cultural management to global leadership: Evolution and adaptation. *Journal of World Business*, 51(1), 115–126.

Cattani, G. (2005). Preadaptation, firm heterogeneity, and technological performance: A study on the evolution of fiber optics, 1970-1995. *Organization Science*, 16(6), 563–580.

Cattani, G. (2006). Technological pre-adaptation, speciation, and emergence of new technologies: how Corning invented and developed fiber optics. *Industrial and Corporate Change*, 15(2), 285–318.

Cheng, C., & Yang, M. (2017). Enhancing performance of cross-border mergers and acquisitions in developed markets: The role of business ties and technological innovation capability. *Journal of Business Research*, 81, 107–117.

Ching, K. (2016). Exaptation dynamics and entrepreneurial performance: evidence from the internet video industry. *Industrial and Corporate Change*, 25(1), 181–198.

Clarke, J. E., Tamaschke, R., & Liesch, P. (2012). International experience in international business research: A conceptualization and exploration of key themes. *International Journal of Management Reviews*, 15(3), 265–279.

108 *An Exaptation Perspective*

Collins, J. D., Holcomb, T. R., Certo, S. T., Hitt, M. A., & Lester, R. H. (2009). Learning by doing: Cross-border mergers and acquisitions. *Journal of Business Research*, 62(12), 1329–1334.

Dew, N., & Sarasvathy, S. D. (2016). Exaptation and niche construction: behavioral insights for an evolutionary theory. *Industrial and Corporate Change*, 25(1), 167–179.

Dew, N., Sarasvathy, S. D., & Venkataraman, S. (2004). The economic implications of exaptation. *Journal of Evolutionary Economics*, 14(1), 69–84.

Dosi, G., & Nelson, R. R. (1994). An introduction to evolutionary theories in economics. *Journal of Evolutionary Economics*, 4(3), 153–172.

Douma, S., George, R., & Kabir, R. (2006). Foreign and domestic ownership, business groups, and firm performance: Evidence from a large emerging market. *Strategic Management Journal*, 27(7), 637–657.

Eggers, J. P., & Kaplan, S. (2013). Cognition and capabilities: A multi-level perspective. *Academy of Management Annals*, 7(1), 295–340.

Gould, S. J. (1991). Exaptation: Tool for an evolutionary psychology. *Journal of Social Issues*, 47(3), 43–65.

Gould, S. J., & Vrba, E. S. (1982). Exaptation: A missing term in the science of form. *Paleobiology*, 8(1), 4–15.

Hendriks, G. (2020). How the spatial dispersion and size of country networks shape the geographic distance that firms add during international expansion. *International Business Review*, 29(6), 101738.

Hymer, S. (1976). *The International Operations of National Firms*. MIT press, Cambridge MA.

Johanson, J., & Vahlne, J. E. (1977). The internationalization process of the firm: A model of knowledge development and increasing foreign market commitments. *Journal of International Business Studies*, 8(1), 23–32.

Jones, G. R., & Hill, C. W. L. (1988). Transaction cost analysis of strategy structure choice. *Strategic Management Journal*, 9(2), 159–172.

Khanna, T., & Yafeh, Y. (2005). Business groups in emerging markets: Paragons or parasites? *Journal of Economic Literature*, 45(2), 331–372.

Kumar, V., Gaur, A. S., & Pattnaik, C. (2012). Product diversification and international expansion of business groups. *Management International Review*, 52(2), 175–192.

Leff, N. H. (1978). Industrial organization and entrepreneurship in the developing countries: The economic groups. *Economic Development and Cultural Change*, 26(4), 661–675.

Luo, Y., & Tung, R. L. (2007). International expansion of emerging market enterprises: A springboard perspective. *Journal of International Business Studies*, 38(4), 481–498.

Mahmood, T., & Mubarik, M. S. (2020). Balancing innovation and exploitation in the fourth industrial revolution: Role of intellectual capital and technology absorptive capacity. *Technological forecasting and social change*, 160, 120248.

Marquis, C., & Huang, Z. (2010). Acquisitions as exaptation: The legacy of founding institutions in the US banking industry. *Academy of Management Journal*, 53(6), 1441–1473.

Meyer, K. E., & Nguyen, H. V. (2005). Foreign investment strategies and sub-national institutions in emerging markets: Evidence from Vietnam. *Journal of Management Studies*, 42(1), 63–93.

Mouritsen, J., Thorsgaard Larsen, H., & Bukh, P. N. (2005). Dealing with the knowledge economy: Intellectual capital versus balanced scorecard. *Journal of Intellectual Capital*, 6(1), 8–27. 10.1108/14691930510574636

Mubarik, M. S. (2015). *Human capital and performance of small & medium manufacturing enterprises: A study of Pakistan* (Doctoral dissertation, University of Malaya). Accessed from: https://core.ac.uk/download/pdf/268878007.pdf (February 2020).

Mubarik, M. S., Govindaraju, C., & Devadason, E. S. (2016). Human capital development for SMEs in Pakistan: Is the "one-size-fits-all" policy adequate?. *International Journal of Social Economics.* 43(8), 804–822.

Mubarik, M. S., Chandran, V. G. R., & Devadason, E. S. (2018). Measuring human capital in small and medium manufacturing enterprises: What matters? *Social Indicators Research*, 137(2), 605–623.

Mubarik, M. S., Devadason, E. S., & Govindaraju, C. (2020). Human capital and export performance of small and medium enterprises in Pakistan. *International Journal of Social Economics*, 47(5), 643–662.

Mubarik, M. S., & Naghavi, N. (2020). Human capital, green energy, and technological innovations: Firm-level analysis. In *Econometrics of Green Energy Handbook* (pp. 151–164). Springer, Cham.

Mubarik, M. S., Bontis, N., Mubarik, M., & Mahmood, T. (2021). Intellectual capital and supply chain resilience. *Journal of Intellectual Capital.* Ahead of print. 10.1108/JIC-06-2020-0206

Mudambi, R. (2008). Location, control and innovation in knowledge- intensive industries. *Journal of Economic Geography*, 8(5), 699–725.

Nachum, L., & Zaheer, S. (2005). The persistence of distance? The impact of technology on MNE motivations for foreign investment. *Strategic Management Journal*, 26(8), 747–767.

Nawaz, R.R., Naghavi, N., Mubarik, M.S., & Reza, S. (2021). Internationalisation challenges of SMEs: Role of intellectual capital. *International Journal of Learning and Intellectual Capital.* 1(1), 1. DOI: 10.1504/IJLIC.2021.10035394

Nelson, R. R., & Winter, S. G. (2002). Evolutionary theorizing in economics. *Journal of Economic Perspectives*, 16(2), 23–46.

Ployhart, R. E., & Moliterno, T. P. (2011). Emergence of the Human Capital Resource: A Multilevel Model. *Academy of Management Review*, 36(1), 127–150. 10.5465/amr.2009.0318

Polhmeier, W., & Ulrich, V. (1995). An econometric model of the two-part decision making process in the demand for health care. *Journal of Human Resources*, 30(2), 339–361.

Reza, S., Mubarik, M. S., Naghavi, N. & Nawaz, R. R. (2021). Internationalisation challenges of SMEs: role of intellectual capital. *International Journal of Learning and Intellectual Capital*, 18(3), 252–277.

Roberts, B. W., Chernyshenko, O. S., Stark, S., & Goldberg, L. R. (2005). The structure of conscientiousness: An empirical investigation based on seven major personality questionnaires. *Personnel Psychology*, 58(1), 103–139. 10.1111/j.1744-65 70.2005.00301.x

Santangelo, G. D., & Meyer, K. E. (2011). Extending the internationalization process model: Increases and decreases of MNE commitment in emerging economies. *Journal of International Business Studies*, 42(7), 894–909.

Santangelo, G. D., & Meyer, K. E. (2017). Internationalization as an evolutionary process. *Journal of International Business Studies* 48(9), 1114–1130.

Santangelo, G. D., & Stucchi, T. (2018). Internationalization through exaptation: The role of domestic geographical dispersion in the internationalization process. *Journal of International Business Studies*, 49(6), 753–760.

110 *An Exaptation Perspective*

Scott, S. G., & Bruce, R. A. (1994). Determinants of innovative behavior: A path model of individual innovation in the workplace. *Academy of Management Journal*, 37(3), 580–607.

Silvia, P. J., Nusbaum, E. C., Berg, C., Martin, C., & O'Connor, A. (2009). Openness to experience, plasticity, and creativity: Exploring lower-order, high-order, and interactive effects. *Journal of Research in Personality*, 43(6), 1087–1090. 10.1016/j.jrp.2009.04.015

Vahlne, J.-E., & Johanson, J. (2017). The internationalization process 1977–2017: The Uppsala model 40 years later. *Journal of International Business Studies*, 48(9), 1087–1102.

Vermeulen, F., & Barkema, H. (2001). Learning through acquisitions. *Academy of Management Journal*, 44(3), 457–476.

Wang, Y., Tang, Y., Yao, X., & Yu, S. (2020). MNE Space and Subnational Location Choice. In *Academy of Management Proceedings* (Vol. 2020, No. 1, p. 10029). Briarcliff Manor, NY 10510: Academy of Management.

Wang, E. Y., & Kafouros, M. (2020). Location still matters! How does geographic configuration influence the performance-enhancing advantages of FDI spillovers?. *Journal of International Management*, 26(3), 100777.

Weyrauch, T., & Herstatt, C. (2017). What is frugal innovation? Three defining criteria. *Journal of Frugal Innovation*, 2(1), 1. 10.1186/s40669-016-0005-y

Winter, S. G., & Szulanski, G. (2001). Replication as strategy. *Organization Science*, 12(6), 730–743.

Zhang, X., Kano, M., Tani, M., Mori, J., Ise, J., & Harada, K. (2018). Hurdle modeling for defect data with excess zeros in steel manufacturing process. *IFAC-PapersOnLine*, 51(18), 375–380.

9 Human Capital, Technological Capabilities, and Productivity: Firm-level Evidence

9.1 Introduction

Over the past two decades, the rapid technological changes have made it imperative for the organization to build dynamic technological capabilities for competing in the highly turbulent business environment. Nevertheless, the development of the latest technological capacities must not be at the expense of reducing the productivity of the existing business operations. The simultaneous pursuit of technological capacities and productivity requires a firm to think out of the box and develop such resource(s), tangible and intangible, that allows a firm to simultaneously pursue the productivity and technology capabilities targets. We argue that human capital could be on intangible resources that simultaneously improve a firm's productivity and technological capacities.

The notion of human capital-led productivity is not new. Several earlier studies could be found highlighting the significant role of human capital in improving productivity. As noted by Mubarik (2015), human capital's impact on productivity can be traced back to the times of Adam Smith (1776), who mentioned human capital an important factor for creating the wealth of a nation. Smith claimed that the investment in educational expenses was as important as the investment in machines. After the Classical times, researchers (e.g., Jacob Mincer 1958; Penrose 1959; Schultz 1961) denoted human capital as the important factor of growth and productivity. Especially, Becker (1962) explained why the investment in human capital was like the investment in other factors of production and how HC mattered for productivity differences. Becker (1962) divided human capital into two terms "specific" and "general". The specific human capital included the skills, knowledge, and abilities to an employer and in general, the skills and knowledge are for all employers. Recent studies (e.g., Männasoo et al. 2018; Mubarik et al. 2018; Hu 2021) have also highlighted an instrumental role of human capital in raising productivity at the micro and macro levels. A brief review of classical and extant literature reveals a direct influence of human capital on productivity. Nevertheless, as to how human capital influence the technological capability of a firm and productivity thereon is a tricky question. Some of the experts are of the view that human capital development is

DOI: 10.4324/9781003195894-9

112   *Firm-level Evidence*

important to uplift the technological capability of a firm. Whereas, others argue that one of the major spillovers of uplifting technological capabilities is human capital development. These contradictory opinions leave the two major questions unanswered. First, what is the relationship of human capital with the technological capability of a firms? Second, does human capital influence a firm's productivity by improving technological capabilities? Addressing these questions can help the firm devise focus policies for productivity enhancement? Against the mentioned backdrop, this chapter empirically tests the role of technological development in the relationship between human capital and productivity. Taking this opportunity, we also examine the effect of HC on a firm's productivity. We have taken Pakistan's manufacturing sector as the case study to test the developed framework. Data has been collected using a close-ended questionnaire from June 2021 to November 2021. The results of the study help to clarify the influence of human capital on the productivity and technological capabilities of a firm. The following section provides the study's theoretical background, followed by hypotheses development.

9.2 Theoretical Background

The study draws its theoretical roots from human capital theory (Becker 1962). As mentioned earlier, Adam Smith (1776) considered education a vital component of the wealth of nations. Likewise, Schultz (1961) used human capital as the important factor of economic growth. Schultz did not give any specific domain or dimension of human capital. Despite of discussion of human capital in classical literature, it was formally theorized by Garry Becker in his seminal work on human capital. Formally, it is known as "human capital theory". Becker (1962) mentioned education, health, and training as human capital and claimed that the investment in human capital like the investment in other factors of production. Becker divided human capital into "specific" and "general". The specific human capital included the skills, knowledge, and abilities to an employer, and in general, the skills and knowledge are for all employers. He mentioned that human capital enhances the prospects of an individual employee and is a source of productivity enhancement for firms. He attributed the rise in productivity and the firm's innovative capabilities to its level of human capital. The concept of Becker was delineated by Wernerfelt (1984) in a resource-based view of the firm (RBV). According to Wernerfelt (1984), resources should have four characteristics: valuable, rare, inimitable, and non-substitutable (VRIN). He mentioned human capital as the factor having the capability of being VRIN. The same was also explained by Penrose (1959). She mentioned managers' experience as the key to combative advantage for the firm. The concept of Becker was further delineated by Romer (1986) and Lucas (1988). Romer (1986) described capital as physical and human capital. Physical capital included factories, machines, tools, and other equipment. Human capital included investment in research and development (R&D),

innovations, or ideas to produce new products that would make the firms competitive and improve performance and productivity. The capital gained by the higher level of education, R&D called "knowledge", might be accumulated through time. The human capital theory states that investment in education is important because it would cause private and social benefits. Private benefits are of individuals they get through a higher level of education or by increasing their skills and capabilities. Social benefits are related to the society, which the overall society gets through the better and developed human capital, causing a prosperous future for the society. Mincer (1996) stated that human capital is a concept that deals with complex and varying definitions. In a context, it may be using education as its indicator with the schooling that may include formal education, while in other contexts, it may deal with health and nutrition as its indicator. The investment in vocational training and other skill-enhancing programs also comes under the definition of human capital. Becker (1993), in his book *Human Capital: A Theoretical and Empirical Analysis,* considered education as a main domain of human capital. He also argued that along with education investment in medical care, computer training courses are also different kinds of capital enhancing productivity. According to Becker, the main dimensions of human capital are medical care (health), training, knowledge-embodied education, and skills. Marimuthu et al. (2009) argued that a person's formal education increases the abilities and skills of the person, resulting in higher earnings and productivity. Severine and Lila (2009),are of the view that the individuals with a higher level of schooling or education are the source of higher economic productivity and the rate of return from education can be calculated and compare of the countries with different income level. Shedding light on education, Kwon and Dae Bong (2009), in the study human capital and its measurement, argued that the education and earning power are correlated to each other; it means that higher the education of the individuals higher is their earnings because education enhances the skills, knowledge, and abilities of the individuals which in turn increase the productivity. Mubarik and Bontis (2022) argued that the organizations could also increase their human capital by enhancing the opportunities of the training, skill enhancement, and knowledge, and organization can be more competitive and productive when its employees are more productive, and they know what is better or valuable for the organization then the productivity of the organization increase.

The aforementioned discussion explains how and why human capital matters for the performance of a firm. It also provides the basis for the proceeding section, which narrows down the performance of the exploration and exploitation activities of the firm and explains their interdependencies.

9.2.1 Human Capital, Productivity, and Technological Capabilities: Theoretical Exposition

Prior studies have highlighted the profound role of human capital resources in uplifting the technological capabilities of a firm. To explain the association

114   *Firm-level Evidence*

between human capital, technological capabilities, and productivity the concept of organizational ambidexterity emphasizes the need to strike a balance between exploratory and exploitative activities of a firm. The focus of the exploitative activities is the refinement of existing processes, knowledge, and expertise, leading to a higher level of productivity (Mubarik and Mahmood 2020). Exploitative activities help reduce the cost of existing business operations and increase present returns (Mahmood et al. 2021). In short, the exploitative activities' overwhelming focus is uplifting organizational productivity. Whereas explorative activities are meant to explore new knowledge, product, or processes. The overarching focus of the explorative activity is innovation in term of processes, products, or technologies. Ferreira et al., (2020, p. 5), *"exploration seems to be more important for achieving differentiated and innovative outcomes, while exploitation is more likely to contribute to cost efficiency and profit gains, efficiency in producing the product, and to its quality"*. We argue that human capital simultaneously improves a firm's productivity (exploitation) as well as technological capabilities (innovation), thus allowing a firm to maintain a balance between both types of activities.

Further, drawing upon the past research (e.g., March 1991; Levinthal & March 1993), we argue that exploration activities provide the foundations for exploitation activities. The exploitation of knowledge can only be done after its creation. Employees uplifting a firm's technological capabilities (exploration) can increase its productivity (exploitation).

9.3 Hypotheses Development

Empirical literature studying the HC-performance relationship has a long history. The study of Schultz (1971) is among the earlier studies on HC-performance relations, finding a positive link between human capital, proxied by education and firm performance. The investment in human capital in the form of education means an enhancement in knowledge which in turn increases labour productivity. During the 90s, many studies attempt to investigate the HC-performance relationship. The work of Lall (1998) is such one prominent study. He stated that there was a positive relationship between human capital and productivity. Psacharopoulos and Patrinos (2004) and Agiomirgianakis et al. (2002) confirmed a positive relationship between education and firm performance. Employees who have specialized skills and knowledge to perform in a better way during complicated tasks. These employees possess special capabilities such as communication and decision-making skills, problem-solving skills, and the capacity to adapt to a continuous learning environment. Youndt and Snell (2004) used data of 208 organizations and found that investment in human capital is more productive as compared to the investment in other forms of capital like physical capital. Bollen et al. (2005) found a complicated relationship between human capital and company performance as it differs with the difference of industries and depends upon the degree of competition. The highly competitive industries have the strongest link between firm performance and human capital.

Here, interesting research of Brunello (2009) is important to cite. The study explored the role of human capital, measured by education, and training (provided by employer organizations in OJT of Thailand. The research demonstrated a significant inverse association between education and training (OJT) and a direct relationship between education and off-the-job training. The findings of these studies are in congruence with the study of Magoutas et al. (2011), who concluded a positive and significant effect of human capital on Greek enterprises. He found that more educated workers are more productive for enterprises and they are enhancing the competitiveness and making them more productive through their capabilities. Olayemi (2012), in a macroeconomic study, investigated the relationship between human capital investment and industrial productivity using 20 years of data from Nigeria. The study used the Granger causality test, co-integration and error correction mechanism (ECM) to examine the relationship between human capital investment and industrial productivity. The study found that there is a positive relationship between education expenditure and industrial productivity in the long run. It means that a higher level of education raises the level of productivity of firms. The study also found a negative relationship between health expenditures and industrial productivity in the long run in the case of the Nigerian economy.

Putting together, a major group of researcher confirm a signifcant impact of human capital on firm's productivity. There are handful of researchers who question the direct role if human capital in improving productivty. They argue that human capital need to be harnessed in the organzational perspective to take the productivity benefits from it. Likewse, there are diverese findings on as to which dimension of human capital improves productivty and how much. Against this backdrop, we draw the following hypothesis.

Hypothesis 1: Human capital improves the productivity of a firm.

Likewise, researchers (Wright et al. 2007; Asif & Lahiri 2021) have demonstrated a profound, significant effect of human capital on technological capabilities. These researchers have operationalized human capital by taking education, training, experience, and skills as the filaments of human capital. The findings of these studies recommend investment in training (both on and off the job) and abilities to elevate the performance-specific human capital. In the same line, Odhon'g and Omolo (2015)) illustrated that the relationship between human capital investment and organizational performance is statistically significant. The study used variables, education, training, knowledge management, and skills developments. Knowledge management and skill development have a significant impact on organizational performance. Human capital investment is an important factor in value creation.

116 Firm-level Evidence

Another aspect of technological capabilities could be examined from research and development (R&D). For example, Erickson and Jacobson (1992) emphasized that research and development have a vital role in gaining an edge over the firms' competitors. It means that the firms that invest more in research and development activities are more competitive and specialized in their specific field. This particular nature of R&D would determine their advantage over other firms. R&D expenditures enable the firms to earn abnormal profits and prevent the imitation of rivals. Likewise, Peter Drucker (2005) stated that the main aim or function of any business is to maximize its profits, and for this purpose they move towards innovation. Innovation provides a competitive edge and hence increases profitability. For this, the businesses invest more resources in R&D activities.

In a nutshell, employees are a rare and valuable source of the business and play a vital role in the failure or success of the business. The training of the employees covers the gap between the desired performance and actual performance of the employees and enhances the workers' productivity.

Hypothesis 2: Human capital improves the technological capabilities of a firm.
Hypothesis 3: Technological capabilities improve the productivity of a firm.

The conceptual framework of the study is exhibited in the Figure 9.1.

From the literature, we have conceived the above framework appearing in Figure 2.1. It shows that human capital, measured by education, health, and skills, is an independent variable affecting productivity. The technological

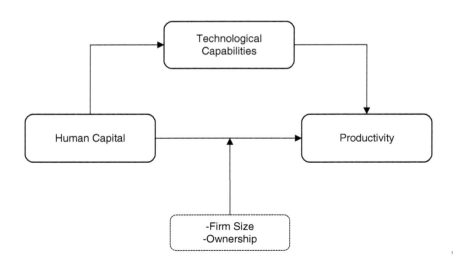

Figure 9.1 Conceptual Framework.

capabilities of the firms are moderating the relationship between human capital and productivity. Two variables, namely firm size and ownership, have been considered control variables. To empirically test this framework, we have selected Pakistan, a prominent South Asian country. The proceeding section unveils the country's background.

9.4 Country Background

To test our framework, we take Pakistan as a case. The 75% share of Pakistan's exports is from the manufacturing sector. Still, the data from 1974–2003 showed a downward trend in the real growth of this sector. Owing to the government's pre-industrial policies, this sector performed remarkably during 50s and 60s, in the early days after the inception of Pakistan. The manufacturing sector growth in 1960s was double-digit, clearly outperforming the rest of the country's sectors. Despite the nationalizations in the 70s and flip-flop policies of subsequent governments, this sector maintained its pace of growth until the 90s. However, in the 90s, the sectoral growth decreased significantly, leaving the economy in a state of ambivalence. In the new millennium, the service sector surpassed manufactirng sector, reducing its contribution from 40% of GDP to 25%. Despite dangling growth, the manufacturing sector's contribution remained substantial in the country's export. From 2008 onward, the country's exports started declining. The present situation is alarming (Mubarik et al. 2021). Owing to this, governments and policymakers are looking to stimulate the manufacturing sector's productivity. Researchers argue that raising this sector's productivity can increase the country's export and provide better employment opportunities. In this context, human capital emerges as a notable option for increasing manufacturing sector productivity.

Despite picking up growth in the last few years, Pakistan's balance of trade is worsening day by day. Declining exports, especially in the manufacturing sector, are significant reasons for the widening trade gap. Several studies have been steered to investigate the reason for declining exports (Mubarik 2015). These studies have exposed energy shortage, tempered infrastructures, and low industrial productivity as the primary reason for declining exports. It is argued that Pakistani exports are not competitive due to high costs and low quality (GOP 2014). Although various factors have been identified and analyzed for their effects on firms' productivity, human capital is a factor that has been less discussed in the empirical literature (Mubarik et al., 2016). The studies, which examined human capital juxtaposed with firm performance, took human capital as an aggregate of education and health missing elements like skills, training, etc. The results of such studies are highly ambivalent and do not provide any conclusive policy guidelines for the manufacturing sector. This also provides an important venue to examine the impact of human capital on productivity by taking a comprehensive and sector-specific measure of human capital. The absence of discussion on the role of firm size and

118   *Firm-level Evidence*

ownership in the relationship of HC-productivity also instigates to add it as moderating variable in the study. Further, several firms in the Pakistani manufacturing sector are expanding their capacity and adopting the latest technological techniques. Such activities are at a peak in Pakistan's steel, cement, sugar, and automotive sectors (Economic Survey of Pakistan 2019). The role of technological interventions in the relationship of human capital—productivity is an important dimension. It can guide the firms to adopt an appropriate policy for elevating their productivity.

9.5 Methodology

9.5.1 Population and Sampling

The targeted population for the subject study is the manufacturing sector firms in Pakistan. Details of the registered will be obtained from the Census of Manufacturing (CMI) industries. The study plans to collect data from 200 manufacturing sector firms.

9.5.2 Data Collection Instrument

The study collected the data with the help of a close-ended questionnaire. The constructs of the variables have been adopted from Mubarik (2015). The questionnaire consists of 40 items; 10 on basic demography of the firms, 7 for HC, 5 for productivity, and 7 for technological capabilities (see Table 9.1).

9.5.3 Analysis Technique

We have employed PLS-SEM to examine the empirical relationship modeled in Figure 9.1. This approach has been preferred due to its robustness against non-normal data and ability to model formative constructs.

9.6 Findings

9.6.1 Respondents Demography

We collected data from 200 firms using the questionnaire discussed above. The data from these firms were collected from June 2021 to November 2021. Table 9.2 briefly illustrates the demography of respondent firms, whereas Table 9.2 demonstrates the demography of individual respondents from the firm. Table 9.2 shows that 200 firms were surveyed, 63 textile firms, 52 leather, 45 sports, and 40 food firms. The majority of the firms (111) are medium firms having an employment size from 100 to 250 as per SBP 2016 definition of medium firms). A few firms (26) are also under foreign ownership. In terms of firm's age, most firms have a life between 10 and 15 years.

Firm-level Evidence 119

Table 9.1 Constructs and their Sources

Construct	Items	Sources
Human Capital	Education	Mubarik (2015);
	Experience (industry-related experience)	Mubarik et al. (2018)
	Skills (level of job-related skills)	
	Training (on the job trainings)	
	Ability (risk-taking ability)	
	Personal traits (interpersonal skills)	
	Compliance	
Technological capabilities	Level of investment in acquiring new technologies	Mubarik (2015)
	Adoption of latest process technologies	
	Uses of contemporary information technologies	
	The ability of radical innovation	
	Level of adoption of ERP	
	The ability of incremental innovation	
Productivity	Compared to competitors our cost of production	Mubarik (2015)
	Compared to competitors, output per worker	
	Level of raw material wastage due to employees	
	Employees manage production processes efficiently	
	Cost per unit as compared to industry leader	

In individual respondents' demography, data reveals that most respondents were managers or senior managers. It is essential to mention that all the respondents were from the human resource, planning, or production department (please see Table 9.3).

9.6.2 Reliability and Validity of Constructs

As discussed in the previous section, the reliability and validity of constructs were ascertained through four steps. First, we check the internal consistency of the construct. It is checked through the value of composite reliability (CR) and Cronbach alpha. The result in Table 9.3 shows that CB alpha and CR values are higher than the threshold levels. Second, Indicator reliability has been assured by checking the factor loading. The results of factor loading in Table 9.3 shows that all items well load on their respective constructs. The factor loading of all items is more than 0.60. Third, convergent validity has been ensured with the help of Average Variance

120   *Firm-level Evidence*

Table 9.2 Respondent Firms Demography

Industry	Number
Textile	63
Leather	52
Sports	45
Food	40
Size	
Medium	111
Large	89
Total	200
Ownership	
Foreign	26
Local	174
Total	200
Age (Years in Operation)	
$\geq$05 years	25
5<age$\leq$10	51
10<age$\leq$ 15 years	86
16< age$\leq$ 20 years	29
Age> 20 years	9

Table 9.3 Respondents Employees demography

Industry	Number
Manager/Senior Manager	83
Deputy Manager	61
Assistant Manager	56
Textile	
Manager/Senior Manager	35
Deputy Manager	24
Assistant Manager	4
Leather	
Manager/Senior Manager	25
Deputy Manager	20
Assistant Manager	7
Sports	
Manager/Senior Manager	10
Deputy Manager	8
Assistant Manager	27
Food	
Manager/Senior Manager	13
Deputy Manager	9
Assistant Manager	18

Firm-level Evidence 121

Extracted (AVE). According to Hair et al. (2006) the value of AVE should be greater than 0.50. Results also show that AVE values of all constructs are greater than 0.50, showing convergent validity. Fourth, the discriminant validity of the construct has been assured by comparing the outer loading with cross-loading (Table 9.4). Results show that all items have higher outer loading than cross-loading, ascertaining discriminant validity. Likewise, the discriminant validity has also been assured by adopting Fornell-Larcker Criteria (Table 9.5).

The VIF statistics show that the multi-Collinearity among variables should be less than three, and all the variables show a VIF less than three in our model; hence, the assumption of collinearity is not violated (Table 9.6).

Table 9.4 Reliability and Validity Statistics

Construct	Items	Factor Loading	AVE	CB Alpha	CR
Human Capital	Education	0.71	0.58	0.83	0.78
	Experience (industry-related experience)	0.69			
	Skills (level of job-related skills)	0.78			
	Training (On-the-job training)	0.81			
	Ability (risk-taking ability)	0.74			
	Personal traits (interpersonal skills)	0.66			
	Compliance	0.83			
Technological capabilities	Investment in acquiring new technologies	0.71	0.52	0.91	0.71
	Adoption of latest process technologies	0.79			
	Uses of contemporary information technologies	0.73			
	The ability of radical innovation	0.72			
	Level of adoption of ERP	0.69			
	The ability of incremental innovation	0.67			
Productivity	Cost of production	0.67	0.51	0.89	0.70
	Compared to competitors, output per worker	0.74			
	Raw material wastage due to employees	0.69			
	Employees manage production processes	0.74			
	Cost per unit as compared to industry leader	0.71			

122 Firm-level Evidence

Table 9.5 Fornell–Larcker Criteria

	Human Capital	Technological Cap	Productivity
human capital	**0.76**		
Technological cap	0.49	**0.72**	
Productivity	0.42	0.38	**0.71**

Table 9.6 Collinarity Statistics (VIF value)

Construct	Item	VIF
Human capital	HC1	1.45
	HC2	1.85
	HC3	1.88
	HC4	1.64
	HC5	1.94
	HC6	1.97
	HC7	1.83
Technological capabilities	TC1	1.72
	TC2	1.65
	TC3	1.56
	TC4	1.44
	TC5	1.88
	TC6	1.96
Productivity	P1	1.82
	P2	1.66
	P3	2.4
	P4	1.78
	P5	2.33

9.6.3 Hypothesis Testing

After ascertaining the validity and reliability, we conduct the hypothesis testing. The results have been exhibited in Table 9.7. The structural model results show that human capital (0.360, $p<0.000$) directly affects firm's productivity. Results also show that human capital (0.17, $p<0.000$) has a profound indirect impact on productivity. It depicts a significant mediating role of technological capabilities in the relationship between human capital and productivity. Studies explain that improvement in human capital improves the employee's ability to contribute in organizational tasks. Thus, this improvement leads toward raising firm's efficacy. Likewise, improving human capital improves organizational ability to adopt new technologies. In fact, an increase in human capital harnesses employees' skills, enabling them to adopt the modern technologies to perform their tasks effectively; therefore, it is strongly recommended to invest in various facets of human capital to improve the firm's performance and technological adaption.

Firm-level Evidence 123

Table 9.7 Path Analysis

Hypothesis	Total Sector	By Size		By Industry			
	Mfg Sector	Medium	Large	Textile	Leather	Food	Sports
Human capital → Productivity	0.27*	0.18*	0.31*	0.57*	0.17*	0.19*	0.39*
Human capital → Technological cap → Productivity	0.48*	0.29*	0.53*	0.71*	0.18	0.21*	0.21*
Human capital → Technological capabilities	0.37*	0.27*	0.61*	0.44*	0.10	0.25*	0.17*
R-square***	0.35	0.37	0.45	0.32	0.25	0.31	0.27
Q-square***	0.34	0.29	0.35	0.21	0.19	0.21	0.33

*, and ** show level of significant at 1%, and 5%
*** Diagnostic tests

The direct coefficients in the path analysis show that the human capital (β = 0.27) has a significant impact on a firm's productivity in the manufacturing sector. Further, when the manufacturing sector is controlled for size; both medium (β = 0.18) and large firms (β = 0.31) showed significant impact on productivity; however, the strength of their coefficients differs. Larger firms showed a higher coefficient (β = 0.31) than medium–sized firms. Similarly, when controlled by industry, the impact of HC remained significant with varying coefficients in different sectors. The textile industry has shown the highest coefficient (β = 0.57) followed by sports (β = 0.39), food (β = 0.19), and leather industry (β = 0.17).

The indirect impact of human capital through mediator shows a significantly positive impact. The results suggest that technological capabilities have a stronger mediating impact in large firms than medium firms. When the manufacturing sector is controlled for the industry, three sectors are found to significantly impact mediation by the technological capabilities on productivity. In contrast, in the leather industry, the effect was found insignificant. Textile (β = 0.71), food (β = 0.21), and sports (β = 0.21) had a positive impact with the highest impact of technological capabilities in the textile sector.

The results of R square show that 35% of the productivity explained by the HC when moderated by technological capability. The explanatory power of the model is between weak and medium. When we consider the size effect, the model explains better for larger firms (0.45) than for medium firms (0.37). However, the model explanatory power ranges from 25% to 32% when industry type is accounted for. The results of Q square show that the overall model has a prediction relevance of 34%, but when accounted for size, large firms have a 35%, and medium firms have 29% predictive

124 *Firm-level Evidence*

relevance. The industry type decomposition decreases the predictive relevance up to around 20%vwith the highest relevance in the textile sector.

9.7 Discussion

Human capital is the main determinant of any industry's success as it enhances the productivity and performance of the industry. Our findings demonstrate that human capital has a positive impact on productivity and firm performance. Nevertheless, there is a difference in the productivity gains from human capital in medium and large manufacturing firms. The overall model used in this paper shows that HC impacts the firm's productivity directly (β = 0.27) and through mediation by a technological cap (β = 0.48). However, the impact of HC increases when there is a role of technological capabilities in the relationship between HC and productivity. The impact of human capital on productivity in a medium-sized industry is lower (β = 0.18) than large organizations (β = 0.31). This difference is due to the available technological capabilities to the human capital, which is a main source of increasing the productivity and performance of firms and individuals. The findings concur with Ramírez et al., (2020). For them, there was a positive impact of human capital on the development of individuals, resulting in the firm's higher productivity. They argue that the investment in human resources in the shape of training and development is the opportunity for long-term productivity. Here, it is essential to mention the study of Beld (2014). Findings also are in line with Beld (2014) study, which examined the effects of R&D investment on firm performance (measured through financial and market-based performance. Beld (2014) also explains that improvement in human capital improves the employee's ability to contribute in organizational tasks. Thus this improvement leads toward raising the firm's efficacy. Likewise, improving human capital improves organizational ability to adopt new technologies. In fact, increase in human capital harnesses employees' skills, enabling them to adopt modern technologies to perform their tasks effectively; therefore, it is strongly recommended invest in various facets of human capital to improve the firm's performance and technological adaption (Mubarik 2015; Ahmed et al., 2019; Mahmood & Mubarik 2020).

The results also suggest that human capital-driven technology leads to firms' innovation and productivity (Capriati & Divella 2017). Investments in human capital further uplifts a firm's technological capabilities that have a greater impact on productivity then the conventional factors. The more a firm invests in technologies and R&D activities, the more it can increase its technological capabilities. That is supported by a positive relation in technological capabilities and productivity in the manufacturing sector of Brazil (Reichert & Zawislak 2014). The other studies also confirmed the positive relationship between technological capabilities and firms' productivity (Wang et al., 2013; Rush et al., 2007). In a nutshell, the findings confirm that organizations can enhance human capital by improving the skills and abilities of their employees.

9.8 Concluding Remarks

The overarching objective of the study was to examine the role of human capital in the simultaneous pursuit of technological capabilities and productivity. The findings from the data obtained from 200 manufacturing sector organizations reveal an instrumental role of human capital in pursuing productivity and technological capabilities together. The findings also bring forth a significant mediating role of technological capacities in the association between human capital and productivity. These findings reflect that human capital improves the technological capabilities, which further improves its productivity.

Since the overarching objective of the study was to demonstrate theoretical linkage of HC and organizational ambidexterity, operationalized as technological development and product, and to initiate the debate on this juxtaposition, it may bear certain limitation in term of generalizability of its empirical findings. This study has been conducted from the data taken from census of manufacturing industries data. The majority of the Pakistani firms do not register in any official databases or systems due to various reasons, including lack of awareness of the system, tax avoidance, or bureaucratic controls. Therefore, CMI data may not be highly representative of all firms, especially those unregistered. We had to use this data as there was no second choice. Therefore, the study results should be generalized with cautious analysis of the context. Sometimes it is also possible that the study results may not be generalized in some sectors. The second major limitation of the study is the use of static data. We collected the cross-sectional data from the firms. The firms' trends may be changed over time, and so may the results. Our results, estimated from cross-sectional data, cannot capture this change. In this regard, collecting the data from the same firms after a year can better view the relationship.

References

Acs, Z. J., & Armington, C. (2004). The impact of geographic differences in human capital on service firm formation rates. *Journal of Urban Economics*, 56(2), 244–278.

Acs, Z. J., & Armington, C. (2006). New firm survival and human capital. In Karlsson C. Johansson B., Stough R. (eds.), *Entrepreneurship and Dynamics in the Knowledge Economy* (pp 125–148). New York: Routledge.

Acs, Z. J., Armington, C., & Zhang, T. (2007). The determinants of new-firm survival across regional economies: The role of human capital stock and knowledge spillover. *Papers in Regional Science*, 86(3), 367–391.

Agiomirgianakis, G., Asteriou, D., & Monastiriotis, V. (2002). Human capital and economic growth revisited: A dynamic panel data study. *International Advances in Economic Research*, 8(3), 177–187.

126 Firm-level Evidence

Ahmed, S. S., Guozhu, J., Mubarik, S., Khan, M., & Khan, E. (2019). Intellectual capital and business performance: the role of dimensions of absorptive capacity. *Journal of Intellectual Capital*, 21(1), 23–39.

Anderson, J. C., & Gerbing, D. W. (1988). Structural equation modeling in practice: A review and recommended two-step approach. *Psychological Bulletin*, 103(3), 411–420.

Antlova, K. (2009). Motivation and barriers of ICT adoption in small and medium-sized enterprises. *E+ M Ekonomie a Management*, 12(2), 140–155.

Aragon-Sanchez, A., Barba-Aragón, I., & Sanz-Valle, R. (2003). Effects of training on business results. *The International Journal of Human Resource Management*, 14(6), 956–980.

Armstrong, M., & Taylor, S. (2014). *Armstrong's Handbook of Human Resource Management Practice*. Kogan Page Publishers, Australia.

Asif, Z., & Lahiri, R. (2021). Dimensions of human capital and technological diffusion. *Empirical Economics*, 60(2), 941–967.

Baptista, R., Karaöz, M., & Mendonça, J. (2014). The impact of human capital on the early success of necessity versus opportunity-based entrepreneurs. *Small Business Economics*, 42(4), 831–847.

Barro, R. J., Mankiw, N. G., & Sala-i-Martin, X. (1995). Capital mobility in neo-classical models of growth. *American Economic Review*, 85(1), 103–115.

Batool, S. A., & Zulfiqar, S. (2011). The performance and structure of small & medium enterprises: An empirical evidence from Pakistan. *Pakistan Journal of Social Sciences*, 31(2), 433–447.

Bayus, B. L., & Agarwal, R. (2007). The role of pre-entry experience, entry timing, and product technology strategies in explaining firm survival. *Management Science*, 53(12), 1887–1902.

Becker, G. S. (1962). Investment in human capital: A theoretical analysis. *Journal of Political Economy*, 70(5, Part 2), 9–49.

Becker, G. S. (1993). Nobel lecture: The economic way of looking at behavior. *Journal of Political Economy*, 101(3), 385–409.

Becker, B. E., Huselid, M. A., Pickus, P. S., & Spratt, M. F. (1997). HR as a source of shareholder value: Research and recommendations. *Human Resource Management*, 36(1), 39–47.

Beld, B. (2014). The effects of R&D investment on firm performance (Bachelor's thesis, University of Twente). Accessed from: http://essay.utwente.nl/66303/

Benhabib, J., & Spiegel, M. M. (2005). Human capital and technology diffusion. *Handbook of Economic Growth*, 1(1), 935–966.

Berry, A., Aftab, K., & Qureshi, S. K. (1998). The potential role of the SME sector in Pakistan in a world of increasing international trade [with comments]. *The Pakistan Development Review*, 5(1), 25–49.

Brooking, A., & Motta, E. (1996). A taxonomy of intellectual capital and a methodology for auditing it. *17th Annual National Business Conference, McMaster University, Hamilton, Ontario*, January 24–26.

Brunello, G. (2009). The effect of economic downturns on apprenticeships and initial workplace training: a review of the evidence. *Empirical Research in Vocational Education and Training*, 1(2), 145–171.

Bollen, L., Vergauwen, P., & Schnieders, S. (2005). Linking intellectual capital and intellectual property to company performance. *Management Decision*, 43(9), 1161–1185.

Capelleras, J.-L., & Rabetino, R. (2008). Individual, organizational and environmental determinants of new firm employment growth: Evidence from Latin America. *International Entrepreneurship and Management Journal*, 4(1), 79–99.

Capriati, M., & Divella, M. (2017). Work organisation, human capital and innovation strategies: new evidence from firm-level Italian data (No. 97). GLO Discussion Paper. Accessed from: https://www.econstor.eu/bitstream/10419/167333/1/GLO-DP-0097.pdf

Carpenter, M. A., Sanders, W. G., & Gregersen, H. B. (2001). Bundling human capital with organizational context: The impact of international assignment experience on multinational firm performance and CEO pay. *Academy of Management Journal*, 44(3), 493–511.

Chowdhury, S. Schulz, E., Milner, M., & Van De Voort, D. (2014) Core employee based human capital and revenue productivity in small firms: An empirical investigation, *Journal of Business Research*, 67 (11), 2473–2479

Coff, R., & Kryscynski, D. (2011). Invited editorial: Drilling for micro-foundations of human capital–based competitive advantages. *Journal of Management*, 37(5), 1429–1443.

Das, A., Handfield, R. B., Calantone, R. J., & Ghosh, S. (2000). A contingent view of quality management: The impact of international competition on quality. *Decision Sciences*, 31(3), 649–690.

Dearden, L., Reed, H., & Van Reenen, J. (2006). The impact of training on productivity and wages: Evidence from British panel data. *Oxford Bulletin of Economics and Statistics*, 68(4), 397–421.

Delery, J. E., & Shaw, J. D. (2001). The strategic management of people in work organizations: Review, synthesis, and extension. *Research in Personnel and Human Resources Management*, 20(1), 165–197.

Deneulin, S., & Shahani, L. (Eds.). (2009). An introduction to the human development and capability approach: Freedom and agency. *IDRC*.

Dessler, G. (2001). *Management: Leading People and Organizations in the 21st Century*. New York, Prentice Hall.

Drucker, P. F. (2005). Managing oneself. *Harvard Business Review*, 83(1), 100–109.

Dzinkowski, R. (2000). The measurement and management of intellectual capital: An introduction. *Management Accounting*, 78(2), 32–36.

Erickson, G., & Jacobson, R. (1992). Gaining comparative advantage through discretionary expenditures: The returns to R&D and advertising. *Management Science*, 38(9), 1264–1279.

Ferreira, J., Coelho, A., & Moutinho, L. (2020). Dynamic capabilities, creativity and innovation capability and their impact on competitive advantage and firm performance: The moderating role of entrepreneurial orientation. *Technovation*, 92, 102061.

Fernández-Mesa, A., & Alegre, J. (2015). Entrepreneurial orientation and export intensity: Examining the interplay of organizational learning and innovation. *International Business Review*, 24(1), 148–156.

Government of Pakistan, Planning Commission. (2014). Pakistan 2025 onenation-one mission. Retrieved from: http://pakistan2025.org/wp-content/uploads/2014/08/Pakistan-Vision-2025.pdf (Accessed: January 09, 2015)

Government of Pakistan[GoP]. (2019). Economic survey of Pakistan. Islamabad: Economic Advisor's Wing Ministry of Finance.

Hair, J., Black, W., Babin, B., Anderson, R., & Tatham, R. (2006). *Multivariate Data Analysis* (7th ed.). Prentice-Hall, Inc., New Jersey.

128 *Firm-level Evidence*

Hu, G. G. (2021). Is knowledge spillover from human capital investment a catalyst for technological innovation? The curious case of fourth industrial revolution in BRICS economies. *Technological Forecasting and Social Change*, 162, 120327.

Javalgi R. G., & Todd, P. R. (2011) Entrepreneurial orientation, management commitment, and human capital: The internationalization of SMEs in India. *Journal of Business Research*, 64 (9), 1004–1010.

Kwon, D. B. (2009, October). Human capital and its measurement. In *The 3rd OECD world forum on 'statistics, knowledge and policy' charting progress, building visions, improving life* (pp. 27–30).

Lall, S. (1998). Technology and human capital in maturing Asian countries. *Science, Technology and Society*, 3(1), 11–48.

Levinthal, D. A., & March, J. G. (1993). The myopia of learning. *Strategic Management Journal*, 14(S2), 95–112.

Lucas, R. E. (1988). On the Mechanics of Economic Development. *Journal of Monetary Economics*, 22, 3–42.

Magoutas, A., Agiomirgianakis, G., & Papadogonas, T. (2011). Education and firm performance. Empirical evidence from Greece. *International Journal of Economic Research*, 8(2), 141–152.

Mahmood, T., & Mubarik, M. S. (2020). Balancing innovation and exploitation in the fourth industrial revolution: Role of intellectual capital and technology absorptive capacity. *Technological Forecasting and Social Change*, 160, 120248.

Mahmood, T., Mubarik, M. S., Islam, T., & Naghavi, N. (2021). Ambidextrous intellectual capital (AIC): a measuring framework. In *The Dynamics of Intellectual Capital in Current Era* (pp. 1–30). Springer, Singapore.

March, J. G. (1991). Exploration and exploitation in organizational learning. *Organization Science*, 2(1), 71–87.

Männasoo, K., Hein, H., & Ruubel, R. (2018). The contributions of human capital, R&D spending and convergence to total factor productivity growth. *Regional Studies*, 52(12), 1598–1611.

Marimuthu, M., Arokiasamy, L., & Ismail, M. (2009). Human capital development and its impact on firm performance: Evidence from developmental economics. *Journal of International Social Research*, 2(8).

Mincer, J. (1957). A study of personal income distribution. Columbia University.

Mincer, J. (1996). Economic development, growth of human capital, and the dynamics of the wage structure. *Journal of Economic Growth*, 1(1), 29–48.

Mubarik, M. S. (2015). Human capital and performance of small & medium manufacturing enterprises: a study of Pakistan (Doctoral dissertation, University of Malaya). Accessed from: https://core.ac.uk/download/pdf/268878007.pdf (February 2020).

Mubarik, M. S., & Bontis, N. (2022). Intellectual capital, leadership and competitive advantage: a study of the Malaysian electrical and electronics industry. *International Journal of Learning and Intellectual Capital*. Ahead of print. Accessed from: https://www.researchgate.net/profile/Muhammad-Mubarik-2/publication/356484928_Intellectual_capital_leadership_and_competitive_advantage_a_study_of_the_Malaysian_electrical_and_electronics_industry/links/62035c753b8968353d340def/Intellectual-capital-leadership-and-competitive-advantage-a-study-of-the-Malaysian-electrical-and-electronics-industry.pdf

Mubarik, M. S., Bontis, N., Mubarik, M., & Mahmood, T. (2021). Intellectual capital and supply chain resilience. *Journal of Intellectual Capital*. Ahead of print. https://doi.org/10.1108/JIC-06-2020-0206

Mubarik, M. S., Chandran, V. G. R., & Devadason, E. S. (2018). Measuring human capital in small and mediummanufacturing enterprises: what matters? *Social Indicators Research*, 137(2), 605–623.

Mubarik, M. S., Govindaraju, C., & Devadason, E. S. (2016). Human capital development for SMEs in Pakistan: is the "one-size-fits-all" policy adequate? *International Journal of Social Economics*, 43(8), 804–822.

Odhon'g, E. A., & Omolo, J. (2015). Effect of human capital investment on organizational performance of pharmaceutical companies in Kenya. *Journal of Human Resource Management*, 3(6), 1–29.

Olayemi, S. O. (2012). Human capital investment and industrial productivity in Nigeria. *International Journal of Humanities and Social Science*, 2(16), 298–307.

Pennings, J. M., Lee, K., & Van Witteloostuijn, A. (1998). Human capital, social capital, and firm dissolution. *Academy of Management Journal*, 41(4), 425–440.

Penrose, E. T. (1959). *The Theory of the Growth of the Firm*. JohnWiley, New York.

Psacharopoulos, G., & Patrinos*, H. A. (2004). Returns to investment in education: a further update. *Education Economics*, 12(2), 111–134.

Ramírez, S., Gallego, J., & Tamayo, M. (2020). Human capital, innovation and productivity in Colombian enterprises: a structural approach using instrumental variables. *Economics of Innovation and New Technology*, 29(6), 625–642.

Rauch, A., Frese, M., & Utsch, A. (2005). Effects of human capital and long-term human resources development and utilization on employment growth of small-scale businesses: A causal analysis. *Entrepreneurship Theory and Practice*, 29(6), 681–698.

Reichert, F. M., & Zawislak, P. A. (2014). Technological capability and firm performance. *Journal of Technology Management & Innovation*, 9(4), 20–35.

Romer, P. M. (1986). Increasing returns and long-run growth. *Journal of Political Economy*, 94(5), 1002–1037.

Rush, H., Bessant, J., & Hobday, M. (2007). Assessing the technological capabilities of firms: developing a policy tool. *R&d Management*, 37(3), 221–236.

Schultz, T. W. (1961). Investment in human capital. *The American economic review*, 51(1), 1–17.

Schultz, T. W. (1971). Investment in human capital. The role of education and of research. The Free Press, A Division of The Macmillan Company, 866 Third Avenue, New York, New York, 10022.

Simonen, J., & McCann, P. (2008). Firm innovation: The influence of R&D co-operation and the geography of human capital inputs. *Journal of Urban Economics*, 64(1), 146–154.

Singapore, S. (2011). *A Guide to Productivity Measurement*. Spring, Singapore.

Skaggs, B. C., & Youndt, M. (2004). Strategic positioning, human capital, and performance in service organizations: A customer interaction approach. *Strategic Management Journal*, 25(1), 85–99.

Slater, S. F., & Narver, J. C. (2000). Intelligence generation and superior customer value. *Journal of the Academy of Marketing Science*, 28(1), 120–127.

Slaughter, S. A., Ang, S., & Fong Boh, W. (2007). Firm-specific human capital and compensation organizational tenure profiles: An archival analysis of salary data for it. *Human Resource Management*, 46(3), 373–394.

130 Firm-level Evidence

Small and Medium Enterprise Development Authority. (2013). *SME sector genesis, challenges and prospects*. SMEDA, Islamabad, Pakistan. Available at: http://www.smeda.org/index.php?option=com_phocadownload&view=category&id=46&Itemid=566 (Accessed December 10, 2014).

Small and Medium Enterprise Development Authority. (2011). *SME development report 2010-11*. SMEDA, Islamabad, Pakistan. Available from: http://www.smeda.org/index.php?option=com_phocadownload&view=category&id=46&Itemid=566 (Accessed May 16, 2014).

Small and Medium Enterprise Development Authority (SMEDA) (2013). *SME sector genesis, challenges and prospects*. SMEDA, Islamabad, Pakistan. Available at: http://www.smeda.org/index.php?option=com_phocadownload&view=category&id=46&Itemid=566 (Accessed December 10, 2014).

Smith, A. (1937). *The Wealth of Nations [1776] Cannan edition*. New York: ModernLibrary.

Syed, A. A. S. G., Ahmadani, M. M., Shaikh, N., & Shaikh, F. M. (2012). Impact analysis of SMEs sector in economic development of Pakistan: A case of Sindh. *Journal of Asian Business Strategy*, 2(2), 44–53.

Tamkin, P., Giles, L., Campbell, M., & Hillage, J. (2004). *Skills Pay: The Contribution of Skills to Business Success*. Institute for Employment Studies, Wahington, DC.

Wang, C. H., Lu, Y. H., Huang, C. W., & Lee, J. Y. (2013). R&D, productivity, and market value: An empirical study from high-technology firms. *Omega*, 41(1), 143–155.

Wernerfelt, B. (1984). A resource-based view of the firm. *Strategic Management Journal*, 5(2), 171–180.

World Bank. (2007). *Enterprise Surveys 2007*. International Finance Corporation, Washington, DC, Retrieved from: http://www.enterprisesurveys.org/~/media/GIAWB/EnterpriseSurveys/Documents/Profiles/English/pakistan-2007.pdf (Accessed December 10, 2014).

Wright, P. M., & McMahan, G. C. (2011). Exploring human capital: putting 'human' back into strategic human resource management. *Human Resource Management Journal*, 21(2), 93–104.

Wu, A. (2005). The integration between balanced scorecard and intellectual capital. *Journal of Intellectual Capital*, 6(2), 267–284.

Youndt, M. A., & Snell, S. A. (2004). Human resource configurations, intellectual capital, and organizational performance. *Journal of Managerial Issues*, 16(3), 337–360.

Zwick, T. (2006). The impact of training intensity on establishment productivity. *Industrial Relations: A Journal of Economy and Society*, 45(1), 26–46.

Zwick, T. (2007). Apprenticeship Training in Germany-Investment or productivity driven? Centre for European Economic Research Discussion Paper No. 07–023. Available at SSRN: http://ssrn.com/abstract=985868

Annexure: Cross-loading

Items	Human Capital	Technological Capabilities	Productivity
HC1	**0.71**	0.51	0.46
HC2	**0.69**	0.49	0.44
HC3	**0.78**	0.58	0.53

(Continued)

Items	Human Capital	Technological Capabilities	Productivity
HC4	**0.806**	0.61	0.56
HC5	**0.74**	0.54	0.49
HC6	**0.66**	0.46	0.41
HC7	**0.83**	0.63	0.58
TC1	0.42	**0.71**	0.43
TC2	0.54	**0.79**	0.51
TC3	0.48	**0.73**	0.45
TC4	0.47	**0.72**	0.44
TC5	0.44	**0.69**	0.41
TC6	0.42	**0.67**	0.39
P1	0.45	0.48	**0.67**
P2	0.52	0.55	**0.74**
P3	0.47	0.5	**0.69**
P4	0.52	0.55	**0.74**
P5	0.49	0.52	**0.71**

10 Human Capital for Fourth Industrial Revolution: Human Capital 4.0

10.1 Introduction

The fourth industrial revolution (Industry 4.0), introduced in Germany in 2011, is considered the game changer regarding its impacts upon businesses and economies (Mubarik et al. 2021; Kusi-Sarpong et al. 2022). It transmutes the conventional business processes, and cutting-edge technologies are replacing the conventional business processes. It has also accelerated the pace and speed of business transactions manifold. A business transaction that was previously taking many days for execution now could be executed in a few seconds. It allows firms to have digitally driven business processes and value-creating networks and provide real-time information of various business activities. Technologies like block-chain has significantly increased the traceability, security, and transparency of the business processes. Likewise, big data, cyber-physical systems, and the internet of things (IoT) are completely changing the business architecture. These technologies enable self-organized, decentralized, and flexible business structures. Be it a supply chain or its marketing, the impact of the technologies could be equally observed on the customer's preference, buying patterns, and expectations. Industry 4.0 technologies are influencing every facet of a business. Further, a number of researchers (e.g, Li 2016; Li & Herd 2017; Luthra & Mangla 2018; Mubarik et al. 2021; Sanders et al. 2017; Telukdarie et al. 2018) note that the pace of adoption of Industry 4.0 technologies is slow and a number of firms report various kind of challenges while adopting I4.0 technologies. These challenges include lack of digital culture, lack of demonstrated sponsorship from the top management, and poor infrastructure. Above all, one of the major challenges is incompatible human capital. The traditional skills and expertise are getting outdated and irrelevant and getting along with the new technologies; businesses require new skill sets and competencies. Due to the lack of systematic exploration, it is harder to determine as to what kind of human capital is needed to capitalize on Industry 4.0 technologies. The ignorance of such skills has resulted in huge financial losses. A case in hand is Brazil, where the country had to suffer huge losses due to the absence of some crucial skills (Cezarino et al. 2019). As noted by Singh and Modgil (2021), "the key to the

DOI: 10.4324/9781003195894-10

success of industry 4.0 depends on understanding and managing the right human capital skills, aligning key resources accordingly, and managing the entire process". They further argue that substantial efforts are required to identify the type of human capital (skills and abilities) required to effectively adopt and benefit Industry 4.0 technologies.

Against the aforementioned backdrop, this study explores the various human capital skills and dimensions necessary for capitalizing on I4.0 technologies. The study also explores as to how developing one skills influences the other. The study adopts a two-fold approach. In the first stage, a comprehensive literature review is done to identify the relevant HC. In the second stage, with the help of experts' opinions and by applying the analytical hierarchal process (AHP), we prioritize the identified HC dimensions with respect to their importance in I4.0.

10.2 Literature Review

10.2.1 Industry 4.0

The advent of steam power and mechanization laid the foundation of the first industrial revolution. It was followed by the second industrial revolution, where the mass production and assembly line approaches radically transformed the conventional modes of production. The third industrial revolution came in computers, electronics, and digitalization. These developments transmuted both production and consumption patterns. The fourth industrial revolution commonly referred to as Industry 4.0, has already started transmuting the industries with the advent of the internet of things (IoTs), cyber-physical systems, and smart factories. Industry 4.0 have already started impacting businesses and radically transmuting the conventional business processes and modes, in the form of smart factories where smart machines with embedded sensors communicate with each other to perform various tasks with minimal human intervention. Presently, the developments like machine learning, big data, and blockchain technologies are accelerating the pace of Industry 4.0 manifolds.

In the proceeding lines, few of the Industry 4.0 developments are discussed to expose how the human capital requirements could be radically different from the past.

Industrial Internet of Things (IIoT): Most of the physical technologies and machines, *e.g., robots, products, machinery, and devices* being used in Industry 4.0, have RFID tags or sensors, which provide real time information about their performance, location, storage condition, and surroundings, etc. This technology has significantly improved the pace, accuracy, and speed of the business processes like product designs, inventory management, and product tracking and is playing a crucial role in decision making.

Artificial Intelligence (AI) and big data analytics: By virtue of numerous sensors, ERP, IoT, and IIoT, a "big" range, frequency, and amount of data is collected, termed as big data. The big data obtained from these smart

134 *Human Capital 4.0*

products and other sources can play an instrumental role in uplifting the process and processes quality, designing new products, and taking strategic business decisions. As a matter of fact, data is called as goldmine of 21st century. This data can be analyzed using powerful tools of AI and machine learning to extract the useful information and insights for effective decision making and automation

Process and organization integration (horizontal and vertical): I4.0 technologies allow various individual processes to be tightly integrated (horizontal integration) across the whole supply chain. Likewise, it allows vertical integration where various firm layers are integrated, allowing a smooth and agile flow of information across the various departments and processes.

Cloud computing: It allows firms to store data on the clouds—3rd party data storage server—with greater safety and security…

Augmented reality (AR): Another core development of I4.0 is AR, which allows individuals to visualize the various objects like machine parts, assembly, or repair instructions, training like a physical thing. AR is yet in the development phase and is expected to have groundbreaking implications for areas like service quality, maintenance and training, etc.

Aforementioned are a few of the developments that I4.0 is accompanying. It has much more to offer like intelligent assets, intelligent factories, and intelligent products. Nevertheless, to manage this "intelligent" product, processes, and resources, human capital must possess highly relevant, state of the art, and agile skills and abilities.

10.2.2 Industry 4.0 Human Capital

Looking into the artifact of industry 4.0 driven technologies, it can be easily analyzed that it requires different set of skills, abilities, and knowledge (human capital). It is not a human-less system rather the roles and tasks and skills required to perform them have been changed (Gupta et al. 2020). Machines take over the physical and repetitive nature of jobs, whereas the analytical nature of work is expected from employees. The changing nature of jobs requires new skills, and expertise to perform them. It may also require a higher level of inter- and intra-organization cooperation. The cutting-edge dynamics of I4.0 require identifying the skills and abilities to capitalize on amicably. Human capital facets like emotional quotient, intelligent quotient, cognitive skills, and soft skills can play an instrumental role in this context. These skills are essential as they allow individuals to be more flexible, adaptable, and continuous learners (Urciuoli 2008).

Similarly, skills related to the data (all types of data including text, video, audio, etc.) handling, management, and analysis—big data analytical skills—could be important in each functional area of an organization. This type of skill can play an instrumental role in understanding a variety of business-related issues like processes errors, quality patterns, and customer satisfaction (Benesova and Tupa 2017).

Since there are variety of skills essential for Industry 4.0, we have categorized them into the four broader categories: cognitive abilities, technical skills, attitudinal skills, and emotional skills.

a   **Cognitive abilities:** This facet of human capital is defined as the capability of the human mind to comprehend complex ideas, degree of abstract and critical thinking, problem-solving skills, and ability to learn and unlearn from experiences (Gottfredson 1997). The seminal work of Carrol (1993), allowing to draw three strata model, defines three stratum of cognitive abilities. The Carrol (1993) work is considered *"most comprehensive and empirically supported"* and they are psychometric and used extensively in the human resource management theory and practice. The Carrol model—based upon the three stratum theory offered by John Carrol (1993)—categorizes cognitive abilities as a general, broad, and narrow stratum.

The first stratum takes into account the specific or narrow abilities. *For* Carroll, (1993, p. 634), *"narrow* abilities represent greater specializations of abilities, often in quite specific ways that reflect the effects of experience and learning, or the adoption of particular strategies of performance".

The second stratum represents broad abilities, which for Carroll (1993) represents "basic constitutional and long-standing characteristics of individuals that can govern or influence a great variety of behaviors in a given domain" (p. 634).

The third stratum represents the most general or broadest level of ability positioned at the top of the hierarchy in Carrolls (1993) model. This cognitive ability considers stratum II (broad abilities) and stratum I(narrow abilities). It is explained as a g(general) factor involving multi-faceted higher-level cognitive processes.

Drawing from the Carrol model, we extract the following cognitive abilities for their relevance and instrumentality in the Industry4.0 human capital framework.

- Problem–solving skills
- Critical thinking
- Creativity
- Cognitive flexibility
- Situational skills

b   **Digital skills:** These are defined as skills and expertise to effectively capitalize on Industry4.0 technologies. Digital skills are defined as skills and expertise helping to use and effectively capitalize in Idnustry 4.0 technologies. These skills represent the knowledge and skills related to

136   *Human Capital 4.0*

the ICTs and digital devices. UNESCO defines it as, *"range of abilities to use digital devices, communication applications, and networks to access and manage information"*. Such skills, according to UNESCO:

- help people to generate digital products and share it with others, communicate it;
- enable people to create and share digital content; and
- enable to communicate and collaborate to solve issues/problems capitalize on opportunities.

Since the digital revolution is influencing all businesses irrespective of their size, type, origin, and industry, digital skills are appearing indispensable. The most traditional sector, i.e., agriculture, is even extensively using the digital devices and sensors to increase in the process of irrigation, sowing, and harvesting. The use of these latest digital developments is greatly enabling them to be more productive, sustainable, and profitable. Likewise, businesses like real estate, conventionally considered face-to-face business, are extensively using digital developments like virtual walks to show the property to the clients and DocuSign for signing and finalizing the agreements. The process of digitalization has further been accelerated by the COVID-19. According to the anecdotes, the digital transformation which took in few months during COVID could have been possible in many normal years. This discussion reveals that digital skills are now essential human capital traits irrespective of any type of business, no matter in which part of the world it operates.

After a review of the literature, we have extracted the following essential digital skills.

- **Cyber security and data protection:** Ability of a person to take relevant measures to safeguard a single computer or computer system from the hackers. It represents the ability to protect the data and digital transactions from any cyber attacks, etc.
- **Digital legislatives**: Information and understating about relevant cyber laws legislative awareness.
- **Digital business analysis:** The application of cutting-edge digital and analytical skills to investigate and analyze certain problem or opportunity to provide its multi-dimensional view. The provision of an objective, in-depth, and multi-dimensional view of any issue helps organization to make right decisions and choices. This also reflects the ability to create a "digital eco-system" of technologies to adopt digital transformation without any serious disruption(s). This skill also considers data analytics skills, which reflects an individual's ability to collect, structure, organize, and access data by applying the latest cutting edge digtla tools to suggest the best solution of any given problem.

- **Social media skills:** The ability to use the various social media platforms to perform business transactions, resolve various businesses, and capitalize on opportunities.

c **Emotional skills:** The third category of skills are related to EQ, which illustrates the ability if an individual to understanding the emotions, feelings, and mind of others. It also represents a person's ability to express his/her feelings towards people, situations, and/or experience(s). Emotional intelligence stands is the apex emotional skill and is considered as an indispensable part of human capital. Alzoubi and Aziz (2021, p. 4) define it as, "Emotional intelligence is the ability to control or monitor the overwhelming feelings and emotions of a person and redirect them into guidance tools. This controlling ability then becomes a skill of a person".

Another important emotional skill is a human skill, denoted as, *"our ability to relate to one another and refer to aspects such as empathy, compassion, and authenticity. People with strong human skills can form deeper connections with colleagues and customers"* (Lewis 2021). There five major human skills that can significantly leverage the performance of employees at the workplace. These are empathy, communication, adaptability, coaching, and trust-building. Empathy is an individual's ability to put themselves in the shoes of others. In other ways, feeling the feel of others. Communication is another important human skill, which refers to the ability of a person to effectively understand and transmit his/her message to the individual or group of individuals. Communication skills have increased manifold in a post-COVID environment where a large chunk of business activities has been shifted onward. Online workplace now demands more active listening and clear communication skills. Another important human skill that has COVID has reinforced is "adaptability"—the ability of an individual to adopt to the changing environment and scenarios. Adaptability is essential for staying optimistic and resourceful. Likewise, coaching—*a manager's capability to listen guide, and empower others*—and trust building—being dependable—are another significant human skill to be taken care of while capitalizing on Industry 4.0.

In the business environment, almost every employee has to undergo certain negotiations irrespective of the job title or industry in which t(s)he works. Hence, negotiation skills are of paramount importance for all employees of an organization; need for such skills has increased manifold in Industry 4.0 environment as the stronger negotiation can significantly contribute to the inter-organizations collaboration. In addition to the effective understating of planning and strategy, negotiation skills heavily rely upon an individual's communication skills and emotional intelligence (Peter 2010; Naghavi and Mubarik 2019).

Decision-making skills, interalia, are key skills for resolving any business issue to capture any opportunity (Naghavi and Mubarik 2017). These skills allow an individual to use employ logical, human, and emotional skills and abilities to decide about a certain situation.

138 *Human Capital 4.0*

The aforementioned review of the literature allows us to identify the following EI skills important for Industry 4.0.

- Emotional intelligence
- Attitude
- Human skills
- Negotiation skills
- Decision-making skills

d **Attitudinal skills:** The fourth category of skills is attitudinal. The attitude—a psychological state of an individual's mind—is also a very critical emotional skill. Several studies (e.g., Covey 1991) has highlighted the role of attitude in the success or failure of any venture. A positive attitude can turn around very difficult and challenging situations, whereas a passive and negative attitude can result in catastrophes. Highly skillful and talented employees with negative attitude could prove fatal for the organizations. As said by Joyce Meyer, a positive attitude gives an individual's power and ability to control their circumstances rather than circumstances control them.

Time management is an important attitudinal trait. It reflects the ability of a person to plan the assigned tasks and responsibly and complete them within the given time frame. This also shows an individual's sensitivity towards time.

Further, another major attitudinal trait is an individual's ability to co-ordinate with all the relevant stakeholders to perform any task or achieve set objectives. In the post-pandemic virtual reality, it has resumed even greater importance. Likewise, the ability to tolerate any undesired response or outcome and deal it amicably is another essential attitudinal trait. Finally, the ability to learn and keep updating a knowledge base and an individual's service focus mindset are also significant constituents of attitudinal skills (Figure 10.1).

In a nutshell, following are the key attitudinal skills:

- Time management
- Coordination
- Tolerance
- Service focus
- Ability to learn

10.3 Findings and Discussion

The finding of AHP analysis reveal that digital skills (0.33) appear to be the most important HC4.0 attributes, followed by cognitive abilities (0.27), attitudinal skills (0.21), and emotional abilities (0.19). The very reason for

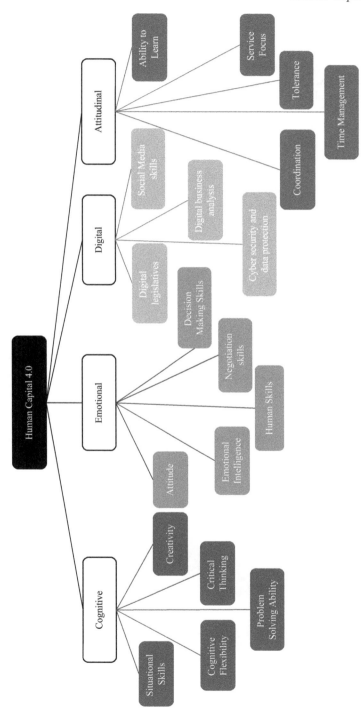

Figure 10.1 HC4.0 Hierarchy.

digital skills to be the most desired among four HC4.0 dimensions, could be seen from the nature and extent of Industry 4.0 technologies. As discussed in the earlier part of this chapter, Industry 4.0 features technologies like internet of things (IoT), industrial internet of things (IIoT), robots, autonomous vehicles, and cyber physical systems. These all technologies require a certain level of digital skills for their effective capitalization. Hence, without digital skills the adoption of Industry 4.0 technologies is onerous (Madonna et al. 2019; Kusi-Sarpong et al. 2022; Mubarik et al. 2021). These findings are also in line with the extant literature. Cognitive skills are just behind the digital skills in term of it importance in Industry 4.0. Although traditional literature considers cognitive abilities essential for technology adoption, its significance was never rated as high as in recent studies. The major cause behind the inflated significance of the cognitive abilities is its high-level instrumentality in the post-COVID business environment. As the COVID pandemic has led to widespread social, psychological, and mental health issues, cognition to understand other perspectives, learn new things, and analyze certain situations truly have resumed high importance (Dirik 2022; Goti et al. 2022). Attitudinal and emotional skills just fall behind cognitive skills but their priority weights are considerably high. Figure 10.2 illustrates their indispensable role in capitalizing on Industry 4.0 technologies.

Although the prioritization of these four skills provide a bird-eye view of the HC4.0, it is essential to see the individual dimensions importance for in-depth understanding. We start from the dimensions of cognitive abilities,

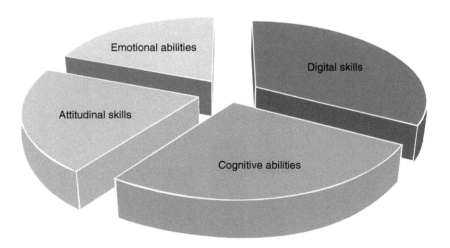

Figure 10.2 Dimensions of HC4.0.

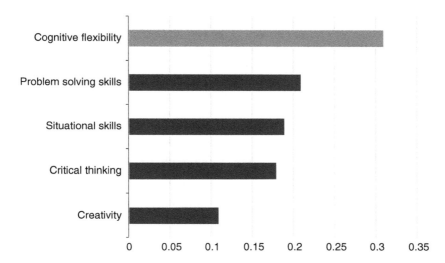

Figure 10.3 Cognitive Abilities.

where cognitive flexibility (0.31) appears to be the most important Cognitive skill in context of Industry 4.0 as exhibited in Figure 10.3. It reflects the ability of individuals to change their behaviour, to be adaptive, according to the changing environment. It has two important facets. First, the ability to think and analyze multiple situations, things, or issues. Second, the ability to mold ones thinking according to the changing conditions (changes in demands, expectations, etc). Huizinga et al. (2006, p. 2019) illustrates the cognitive flexibility as the major human trait for higher performance. The define cognitive flexibility as, "the ability to "shift back and forth between multiple tasks" (p. 2019). Such capability not only allow individuals to adopt latest developments but also permit them to come up with creative ways of dealing with the existing challenges and processes. Problem-solving ability (0.21) appears to be the second important constituent of cognitive abilities. It entails an individual's ability to handle any unexpected or challenging situation and come up with workable solution. In other words, it involves assessment of a situation and coming up with a workable solution without creating any disruption or panic. It may involve the use of an employee's active listening, creativity, and decision-making skills simultaneously. Such skills play significant role in amicable adoption of Industry 4.0 technologies. During adoption phase, numerous challenges, conflicts, and issues appear. In such scenarios, employees' problem solving skills play instrumental role to overcome these challenges and difficulties (Matošková et al. 2020; Xu et al. 2020). Situational awareness or situational skills (0.19), appears to be the next important cognitive ability of employees

142 *Human Capital 4.0*

that can be crucial for Industry 4.0. Mubarik (2015) argue that poor situational skill or awareness can result in tragic and catastrophic situation especially complex environment. Likewise critical thinking (0.18), an ability to actively understand, analyze, and evaluate a given situation, issue, or opportunity and question as to how it could be improved, capitalized, used or avoided. Usually, critical thinkers do not accept the idea, development, and technology at its face rather (s)he thinks about various facets, usage, and loopholes. It is important for technology adoption as any given technology, like Industry 4.0, may not necessarily contribute to the firm and may require some pre-requisite before adoption. Creativity, last in the cognitive flexibly tribe but obviously not least, carries 0.11 weightage, which is quite considerable. It reflects employee's ability to think, and generate novel idea or alternatives that could be used to overcome any issue, capitalize on any opportunity, or improve performance of a function, department, or organization (Mubarik 2015). Employees with creativity could help organization to adopt and use Industry 4.0 technologies in creative and robust way.

Among the dimensions of digital skills, digital business analysis skills (0.40) sits at the top of the list (Figure 10.4).

The findings reveal (positive) attitude (0.26) as the most significant emotional skills. It is closely followed by emotional intelligence (0.24). The role positive attitude in employee's individual performance is well supported by the empirical literature. The differing outcomes of the same situation posed to many people is due to the differing attitude of each individual (Talukder and Galang 2021). We argue that the outcome of individuals in specific situation depends upon their attitude. Similarly, emotional

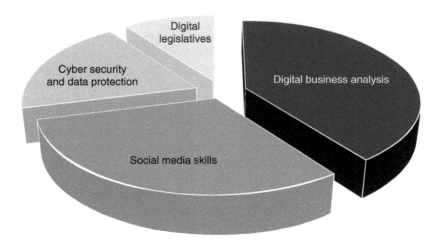

Figure 10.4 Digital Skills.

intelligence, illustrating individual's ability to express their feelings towards people, situation, and/or experience(s), appears as an essential facet of emotional skills. Since businesses rotate around the people, understanding the people's emotions, and non-verbal language is essential. Likewise, it is also important how an individual expresses his/her feeling about particular object, situation, or thing. These two important tasks require strong emotional intelligence, presence of which can significantly help adopt Industry 4.0 technologies.

Further, human skills characterized by empathy, communication, adaptability, coaching, and trust building appear to be third essential pillar of emotional skills. Importance of human skills can never be undermined as absence of these skills can create a catastrophic situation for the organization. For example, empathy, a major human skill, has been dented as a skill which can create a deciding difference in the performance of an employee. Manson (2016) mentioned the case of a business professional, who fell from the heights of success and fame to the bottom of bottoms of failure. He mentioned the lack of empathy— *situation occurred due to the removal of some brain cells dealing with the empathetic behavior of human during the brain surgery of*—as the reason behind the downfall. Other two skills, decision making and negotiations, have important role in the adoption of technologies like Industry 4.0 (Figure 10.5).

Among attitudinal skills, time management (0.31) appears to be the most important followed by the ability to learn (0.25), service focus (0.18) coordination (0.15), and tolerance (0.11). The heightened importance of time management skills, among others, is strongly supported by empirical evidences and number of organization conduct workshops to inculcate the time management skills among their employees. It is considered as one of the pre-requisite for good performance. An individual with poor time management skill can be at the mercy of events and occasions around him, struggling to meet the deadlines. Further, ability to learn, especially in the post-COVID environment where number of transitional operations and ways of doing work have become obsolete are becoming obsolete and new

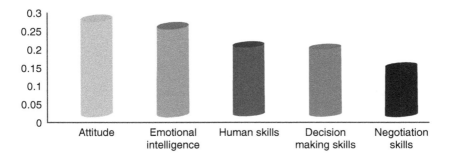

Figure 10.5 Emotional Skills.

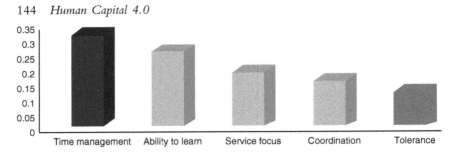

Figure 10.6 Attitudinal Skills.

technologies and developments are rapidly taking place, ability to learn appears to be an essential human capital trait (Jaiswal et al., 2021; Park and Park 2021). Further, our findings exhibit service focus as the third important cord of attitudinal skill. The role of service-oriented attitude could be seen in Singapore. The country hosts the world's best hotels, vibrating financial institutions, best airlines, and best airports. One of the major reasons, according to Ron Kaufman (2012), is their service excellence attitude. Coordination and tolerance are another two important attitudinal skills, which despite of their lesser comparative weightage, assume great role in adopting Industry 4.0 technologies (Figure 10.6).

Table 10.1 and Table 10.2 reflect the consolidated findings of the study and provide a snapshot of the aforementioned discussion.

Table 10.1 Summary of Human Capital 4.0

Dimensions	Sub-dimensions
Cognitive abilities	Problem-solving skills
	Critical thinking
	Creativity
	Cognitive flexibility
	Situational skills
Digital	Cyber security and data protection
	Digital legislatives
	Digital business analysis
	Social media skills
Emotional	Emotional intelligence
	Attitude
	Human skills
	Negotiation skills
	Decision making skills
Attitudinal skills	Time management
	Coordination
	Tolerance
	Service focus
	Ability to learn

Human Capital 4.0   145

Table 10.2 Relative Prioritization of Human Capital 4.0 Dimensions and Sub-dimensions

Dimensions	Weights	Sub-dimensions	LW	GW
Cognitive abilities	0.27	Problem-solving skills	0.21	0.0567
		Critical thinking	0.18	0.0486
		Creativity	0.11	0.0297
		Cognitive flexibility	0.31	0.0837
		Situational skills	0.19	0.0513
Digital	0.33	Cyber security and data protection	0.19	0.0627
		Digital legislatives	0.10	0.033
		Digital business analysis	0.40	0.132
		Social media skills	0.31	0.1023
Emotional	0.19	Emotional intelligence	0.24	0.0456
		Attitude	0.26	0.0494
		Human skills	0.19	0.0361
		Negotiation skills	0.13	0.0247
		Decision-making skills	0.18	0.0342
Attitudinal skills	0.21	Time management	0.31	0.0651
		Coordination	0.15	0.0315
		Tolerance	0.11	0.0231
		Service focus	0.18	0.0378
		Ability to learn	0.25	0.0525
Total	1		4	1

The relative prioritization of HC4.0 dimensions have been exhibited in Figure 10.7. These relative prioritization show digital business analysis, social media skills, and cognitive flexibility as the three leading HC4.0 skills.

10.4 Conclusion and Implications

The aim of this chapter was to identify the most significant general skills for Human Capital 4.0 architecture. We adopted a two-fold approach to reach on the objectives. In the first stage, we reviewed the literature in the human capital in context of Industry 4.0 and identified four major skills and their 20 dimensions (sub-skills). In the second stage, expert's response was recorded using a bi-polar questionnaire, followed by a short interview. The data obtained through bi-polar questionnaire was computed and the AHP was employed to compute the relative importance of HC4.0 skills and their dimensions. The AHP findings reveal the digital skills to be leading among four essential HC4.0 skills, followed by cognitive abilities, attitudinal abilities, and emotional abilities. The comparison of their dimensions reveal digital business analysis, social media skills, and cognitive flexibility as the three leading HC4.0 skills.

These findings imply that a firm should develop its employee's digital business, analysis, social media, and cognitive flexibility skills to adopt Industry 4.0 technologies.

146 Human Capital 4.0

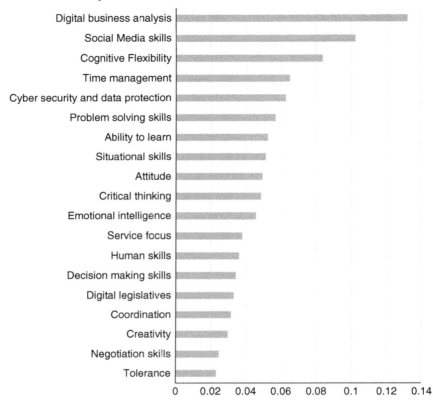

Figure 10.7 Relative Importance of HC4.0.

Acknowledgement

The data collection of this chapter was supported by HEC Pakistan under NRPU 20–11226.

References

Alzoubi, H. M., & Aziz, R. (2021). Does emotional intelligence contribute to quality of strategic decisions? The mediating role of open innovation. *Journal of Open Innovation: Technology, Market, and Complexity*, 7, 130.

Benešová, A., & Tupa, J. (2017). Requirements for education and qualification of people in industry 4.0. *Procedia Manufacturing*, 11, 2195–2202.

Carroll, J. B. (1993). *Human Cognitive Abilities: A Survey of Factor-analytic Studies*. Cambridge University Press. https://doi.org/10.1017/CBO9780511571312

Cezarino, L. O., Liboni, L. B., Oliveira Stefanelli, N., Oliveira, B. G., & Stocco, L. C. (2019). Diving into emerging economies bottleneck: Industry 4.0 and implications for circular economy. *Management Decision*, 59, 1841–1862.

Covey, S. R. (1991). *The 7 Habits of Highly Effective People*. Simon & Schuster, New York.

Dirik, D. (2022). Industry 4.0 and the new world of work. In *Industry 4.0 and Global Businesses*. Emerald Publishing Limited.

Goti, A., Akyazi, T., Alberdi, E., Oyarbide, A., & Bayon, F. (2022). Future skills requirements of the food sector emerging with industry 4.0. In *Innovation Strategies in the Food Industry* (pp. 253–285). Academic Press.

Gottfredson, L. S. (1997). Why g matters: The complexity of everyday life. *Intelligence*, 24(1), 79–132.

Gupta, S., Leszkiewicz, A., Kumar, V., Bijmolt, T., & Potapov, D. (2020). Digital analytics: Modeling for insights and new methods. *Journal of Interactive Marketing*, 51, 26–43.

Hafni, R. N., Herman, T., Nurlaelah, E., & Mustikasari, L. (2020, March). The importance of science, technology, engineering, and mathematics (STEM) education to enhance students' critical thinking skill in facing the industry 4.0. In *Journal of Physics: Conference Series* (Vol. 1521, No. 4, p. 042040). IOP Publishing.

Huizinga, M., Dolan, C. V., & Van der Molen, M. W. (2006). Age-related change in executive function: Developmental trends and a latent variable analysis. *Neuropsychologia*, 44(11), 2017–2036.

Jaiswal, A., Arun, C. J., & Varma, A. (2021). Rebooting employees: Upskilling for artificial intelligence in multinational corporations. *The International Journal of Human Resource Management*, 33, 1–30.

Jiang, J., Gao, A., & Yang, B. (2018). Employees' critical thinking, leaders' inspirational motivation, and voice behavior. *Journal of Personnel Psychology*, 17(1), 33–41. 10.102 7/1866-5888/a000193

Kaufman, R. (2012). *Uplifting Service*. New York, NY: Evolve Publishing.

Kusi-Sarpong, S., Mubarik, M. S., Khan, S. A., Brown, S., & Mubarak, M. F. (2022). Intellectual capital, blockchain-driven supply chain and sustainable production: Role of supply chain mapping. *Technological Forecasting and Social Change*, 175, 121331.

Lewis, A. (2021). *5 Key Human Skills to Thrive in the Future Digital Workplace*, Harvard Business Publishing Corporate Learning. Accessed from: https://www.harvardbusiness. org/5-key-human-skills-to-thrive-in-the-future-digital-workplace/#:~:text=What %20exactly%20are%20human%20skills,connections%20with%20colleagues%20and %20customers. (Jan 2022)

Li, J. (2016). Technology advancement and the future of HRD research. *Human Resource Development International*, 19(3), 189–191.

Li, J., & Herd, A. M. (2017). Shifting practices in digital workplace learning: An integrated approach to learning, knowledge management, and knowledge sharing. *Human Resource Development International*, 20(3), 185–193.

Luthra, S., & Mangla, S. K. (2018). Evaluating challenges to Industry 4.0 initiatives for supply chain sustainability in emerging economies. *Process Safety and Environmental Protection*, 117, 168–179.

Manson, M. (2016) *The Subtle Art of Not Giving a F*ck*. Harper One, New York.

Madonna, M., Monica, L., Anastasi, & Di Nardo, M. (2019). Evolution of cognitive demand in the human–machine interaction integrated with industry 4.0 technologies. *Wit Trans. Built Environ*, 189, 13–19.

Mahmood, T., & Mubarik, M. S. (2020). Balancing innovation and exploitation in the fourth industrial revolution: Role of intellectual capital and technology absorptive capacity. *Technological Forecasting and Social Change*, 160, 120248.

148 *Human Capital 4.0*

Matošková, J., Bartók, O., & Tomancová, L. (2020). The relation between employee characteristics and knowledge sharing. *VINE Journal of Information and Knowledge Management Systems.* https://doi.org/10.1108/VJIKMS-05-2020-0092

Modgil, S., Singh, R. K., & Hannibal, C. (2021). Artificial intelligence for supply chain resilience: learning from Covid-19. ahead-of-print. *The International Journal of Logistics Management.* 10.1108/ijlm-02-2021-0094

Mubarik, M. S. (2015). *Human Capital and Performance of Small & Medium Manufacturing Enterprises: A Study of Pakistan* (Doctoral dissertation, University of Malaya).

Mubarik, S., Chandran, V. G. R., & Devadason, E. S. (2016). Relational capital quality and client loyalty: Firm-level evidence from pharmaceuticals, Pakistan. *The learning organization*, 23(1), 43–60. https://doi.org/10.1108/TLO-05-2015-0030

Mubarik, M. S., Chandran, V. G. R., & Devadason, E. S. (2018). Measuring human capital in small and medium manufacturing enterprises: What matters? *Social Indicators Research*, 137(2), 605–623.

Mubarik, M. S., Naghavi, N., Mubarik, M., Kusi-Sarpong, S., Khan, S. A., Zaman, S. I., & Kazmi, S. H. A. (2021). Resilience and cleaner production in industry 4.0: Role of supply chain mapping and visibility. *Journal of Cleaner Production*, 292, 126058.

Naghavi, N., & Mubarik, M. S. (2019). Negotiating with managers from South Asia: India, Sri Lanka, and Bangladesh. In *The Palgrave Handbook of Cross-Cultural Business Negotiation* (pp. 487–514). Palgrave Macmillan, Cham.

O'Brien, K. S., & O'Hare, D. (2007). Situational awareness ability and cognitive skills training in a complex real-world task. *Ergonomics*, 50(7), 1064–1091.

Park, S., & Park, S. (2021). How can employees adapt to change? Clarifying the adaptive performance concepts. *Human Resource Development Quarterly*, 32(1), E1–E15.

Peter, O. I., Abiodun, A. P., & Jonathan, O. O. (2010). Effect of constructivism instructional approach on teaching practical skills to mechanical related trade students in western Nigeria technical colleges. *International NGO Journal*, 5(3), 59–64.

Sanders, A., K Subramanian, K. R., Redlich, T., & Wulfsberg, J. P. (2017, September). Industry 4.0 and lean management–synergy or contradiction?. In *IFIP International Conference On Advances In Production Management Systems* (pp. 341–349). Springer, Cham.

Telukdarie, A., Buhulaiga, E., Bag, S., Gupta, S., & Luo, Z. (2018). Industry 4.0 implementation for multinationals. *Process Safety and Environmental Protection*, 118, 316–329.

Talukder, A. M. H., & Galang, M. C. (2021). Supervisor support for employee performance in Australia: Mediating role of work-life balance, job, and life attitude. *Journal of Employment Counseling*, 58(1), 2–22.

Urciuoli, B. (2008). Skills and selves in the new workplace. *American ethnologist*, 35(2), 211–228.

Xu, Y., Shieh, C. H., van Esch, P., & Ling, I. L. (2020). AI customer service: Task complexity, problem-solving ability, and usage intention. *Australasian Marketing Journal (AMJ)*, 28(4), 189–199.

Human Capital 4.0 149

Questionnaire

Please compare the relative importance of following dimensions with respect to the Human Capital 4.0:

Dimensions	Scale	Dimensions
	9 8 7 6 5 4 3 2 1 2 3 4 5 6 7 8 9	
Cognitive abilities		Digital
Cognitive abilities		Emotional
Cognitive abilities		Attitudinal skills
Digital		Emotional
Emotional		Attitudinal skills

Please compare the relative importance of following dimensions with respect to the dimensions mentioned in the extreme right:

Dimensions	Sub-dimensions	Scale	Sub-dimensions
Cognitive abilities	Problem-solving skills	9 8 7 6 5 4 3 2 1 2 3 4 5 6 7 8 9	Critical thinking
	Problem-solving skills		Creativity
	Problem-solving skills		Cognitive flexibility
	Problem-solving skills		Situational skills
	Critical thinking		Creativity
	Critical thinking		Cognitive flexibility
	Critical thinking		Situational skills
	Cognitive flexibility		Situational skills
	Cognitive flexibility		Creativity
	Situational skills		Creativity
Digital	Cyber security and data protection		Digital legislatives
	Cyber security and data protection		Digital business analysis
	Cyber security and data protection		Social media skills
	Digital legislatives		Digital business analysis
	Digital legislatives		Social media skills
	Digital business analysis		Social media skills
Emotional	Emotional intelligence		Attitude
	Emotional intelligence		Human skills
	Emotional intelligence		Negotiation skills
	Emotional intelligence		Decision-making skills
	Attitude		Human skills
	Attitude		Negotiation skills
	Attitude		Decision-making skills
	Human skills		Negotiation skills
	Human skills		Decision-making skills
	Negotiation skills		Decision-making skills
	Time management		Coordination

(Continued)

150 Human Capital 4.0

Dimensions	Sub-dimensions	Scale		Sub-dimensions
Attitudinal	Time management			Tolerance
skills	Time management			Service focus
	Time management			Ability to learn
	Coordination			Tolerance
	Coordination			Service focus
	Coordination			Ability to learn
	Tolerance			Service focus
	Tolerance			Ability to learn
	Service focus			Ability to learn

Index

accounting oriented approach 16
AHP 19, 20, 37, 45, 46, 133, 138, 145
ambidextrous learning 50, 51, 52, 60–62
ambivalent results 25
attitudinal skills 135, 138, 143, 144, 145, 147, 150

balance score card 19
behavioral human capital 79–81, 85–87, 91, 93
block-chain 132

Chicago School Economists 3, 6
cognitive abilities 58, 135, 138, 140, 144, 145
cross-border acquisitions 38, 40

definitions of human capital 4–6
disruptive technologies 1, 50
double-layered acculturation 42, 101, 104

evolution of human capital
exaptive human capital 106
exaptation 42, 99, 101–103, 105–107
exploitative 56, 114

firm level human capital 65–67
franchising 38, 39, 43

general human capital 5, 52

human capital and internationalization 37, 41, 105
human capital development 7, 46, 50
human capital development strategies 50–52, 62
Human Capital Index 20

human capital monitor 20
human capital readiness 26, 27, 29, 32–34
human capital readiness spectrum 34
human capital resource 8, 51, 54–56, 61, 65–67, 69, 70, 71, 73, 75, 76, 82, 85, 99, 10, 106, 113
human capital strategist 1
human capital theory 6, 7,42, 51, 79, 100, 112, 113

indicators based approaches 13
individual level human capital 66–68
Industry 4.0 human capital 134
Industry 4.0 135, 137, 138, 140–145
innovative work behavior 65–68, 71–75

joint venture 38, 39, 101, 104

Knightian Uncertainty 106, 107
KSA 3, 7,12, 27, 52, 53, 60, 80

M&A(mergers and acquisitions) 37, 38, 46
macro measurement approaches of HC 13
market return approaches 19
market value approach 16
micro measurement approaches 15
monetary based approaches 13

negotiation skills 43, 44, 48, 49, 137, 139, 143–146

OJT 17, 115
The Organizational Performance Model Of Mercer HR Consulting 20

The Post -WWII Era And Human Capital 2

152 *Index*

potential absorptive capacity 83, 85, 87–90
problem with the traditional human capital 21

RBV (resource base view) 21, 51, 84, 100, 112
realized absorptive capacity 83, 85, 87–90
relational climate 50–52, 57, 58, 59–62
research and development 112, 116
role of human capital 1, 3, 7, 25, 37, 65, 73, 75, 79, 87, 111, 113, 115, 125

SMEs 87, 88, 93
specific human capital 21, 30, 42, 53, 99, 105, 111, 112, 115

talent management 53–55, 58, 59, 61, 62
time management 138, 143–146, 148–150
types of internationalization 37, 38

value added approaches 19
VRIN 112

Milton Keynes UK
Ingram Content Group UK Ltd.
UKHW031503071224
451979UK00020B/214